Getting Started

Learn effective ways to teach STEAM with this helpful book from educational technology experts Billy Krakower and Meredith Martin. Whether you have a dedicated STEAM class, or plan to integrate it into a regular classroom, you'll find out how to create a structured learning environment while still leaving room for inquiry and innovation. You'll also gain a variety of hands-on activities and rubrics you can use immediately.

Topics include:

- the differences among STEM, STEAM, and makerspaces
- planning your STEAM space
- stocking your space with the right supplies
- planning for instruction and managing class time
- incorporating the core subjects
- aligning lessons with standards and assessments
- getting the administration and community involved
- taking your class to the next level with design thinking.

With this practical book, you'll have all the tools you'll need to create a STEAM-friendly learning space starting now.

Continue the conversation on Twitter with the hashtag #GSwSTEAM!

Billy Krakower is an internationally recognized education speaker, trainer, and author of several books including *Connecting Your Students with the World* (with Jerry Blumengarten and Paula Naugle). He can be found at www.billykrakower.com and followed on Twitter @wkrakower.

Meredith Martin is an educator of over 20 years, and a national speaker and consultant on a variety of educational topics. She is a Google Certified Educator and Innovator, and has a passion for STEM, STEAM, makerspaces, and project based learning. She can be found online at www.techforteachers.com and on Twitter @geekyteach.

Also Available from Routledge Eye On Education
(www.routledge.com/eyeoneducation)

Connecting Your Students with the World: Tools and Projects to Make Global Collaboration Come Alive, K–8
Billy Krakower, Paula Naugle, and Jerry Blumengarten

Global Concepts for Young People: Stories, Lessons, and Activities to Teach Children About Our World
Becky Hunt

Intentional Innovation: How to Guide Risk-Taking, Build Creativity Capacity, and Lead Change
A.J. Juliani

STEM by Design: Strategies and Activities for Grades 4–8
Anne Jolly

Creating Scientists: Teaching and Assessing Science Practice for the NGSS
Christopher Moore

The Genius Hour Guidebook: Fostering Passion, Wonder, and Inquiry in the Classroom
Denise Krebs and Gallit Zvi

Passionate Learners, 2nd Edition: How to Engage and Empower Your Students
Pernille Ripp

Your First Year: How to Survive and Thrive as a New Teacher
Todd Whitaker, Katherine Whitaker, and Madeline Whitaker

Getting Started with STEAM

Practical Strategies for the K–8 Classroom

Billy Krakower and Meredith Martin

Routledge
Taylor & Francis Group
NEW YORK AND LONDON

First published 2019
by Routledge
711 Third Avenue, New York, NY 10017

and by Routledge
2 Park Square, Milton Park, Abingdon, Oxon, OX14 4RN

Routledge is an imprint of the Taylor & Francis Group, an informa business

© 2019 Taylor & Francis

The right of Billy Krakower and Meredith Martin to be identified as authors of this work has been asserted by them in accordance with sections 77 and 78 of the Copyright, Designs and Patents Act 1988.

All rights reserved. No part of this book may be reprinted or reproduced or utilised in any form or by any electronic, mechanical, or other means, now known or hereafter invented, including photocopying and recording, or in any information storage or retrieval system, without permission in writing from the publishers.

Trademark notice: Product or corporate names may be trademarks or registered trademarks, and are used only for identification and explanation without intent to infringe.

Library of Congress Cataloging-in-Publication Data
Names: Krakower, Billy, author. | Martin, Meredith (Educational trainer), author.
Title: Getting started with STEAM : practical strategies for the K-8 classroom / Billy Krakower, Meredith Martin.
Description: New York, NY : Routledge, 2018. | Includes bibliographical references and index.
Identifiers: LCCN 2018009745 | ISBN 9781138586628 (hbk : alk. paper) | ISBN 9781138586635 (pbk : alk. paper) | ISBN 9780429504501 (ebk)
Subjects: LCSH: Science–Study and teaching (Elementary) | Science–Study and teaching (Middle school) | Arts–Study and teaching (Elementary) | Arts–Study and teaching (Middle school) | Science and the arts. | Creative activities and seat work.
Classification: LCC LB1585 .K697 2018 | DDC 372.35/044–dc23
LC record available at https://lccn.loc.gov/2018009745

ISBN: 978-1-138-58662-8 (hbk)
ISBN: 978-1-138-58663-5 (pbk)
ISBN: 978-0-429-50450-1 (ebk)

Typeset in Palatino
by Swales & Willis Ltd, Exeter, Devon, UK

Visit the eResources: www.routledge.com/9781138586635

To Jim and Carol Baldino, who always provide support and love no matter what crazy ideas I have. And to my SLAMS family for making my 'day job' the best in the world!

– Meredith

To Jennifer, who always supports me no matter how crazy my ideas might become or how long I will be working on a lesson. To Brianna who makes me smile and laugh daily and reminds me that you can always explore new ways to complete a task.

– Billy, or Daddy

Contents

    eResources ix
    Meet the Authors... x
    Preface xi

1 The What and Why of STEAM 1
    The Jargon Jungle: Makers, STEM, and STEAM – What's
    the Difference? 1
    Now You Have the WHAT, Let's Find Out the WHY 6
    Technology Is Not Just Computers 8

2 Planning Your STEAM Space 11
    Introduction 11
    What Does a Dedicated Space Look Like? 11
    What Does STEAM Look Like Integrated
    into Classrooms?... 15
    Other Spaces and Ways to Incorporate STEAM................... 16
    Making and STEAM, a Perfect Combination 19

3 Stocking Your Space: What Supplies Do You Need? 21
    Don't Break the Bank: Dollar Store STEAM Supplies 21
    Inexpensive Electronics 23
    A Well-stocked Toolkit 25
    Let's Splurge a Little....................................... 26
    Grants, Donations, and Other Ways
    to Stock Your Space 28

4 Planning for Instruction 31
    How Do I Plan a STEAM Lesson? 31
    Managing My Time with a Tight Schedule....................... 37
    Student-Centered Lesson...................................... 38

5 Incorporating the Core Subjects 41
    Incorporating Language Arts (Writing and Reading) into STEAM.. 41
    Incorporating Technology..................................... 44
    Incorporating the Arts 45

Incorporating Engineering 46
Incorporating Social Studies 48
Incorporating Math 48

6 Getting Aligned: Standards and Assessments 53
ISTE Standard 4. Innovative Designer 55
Assessment 55

7 It Takes a Village: Getting the Community Involved 59
Administration 59
Family 63
Community 64

8 Design Thinking: Taking Your STEAM Class to the Next Level 67
Changing Your Thinking with Empathy 67
Ready, Set, Design! 69
Extraordinary Design 71

9 Next Steps 75
Where Do We Go from Here? 75
Takeaways and Resources 75

10 Conclusion 81

Appendix: Sample Projects and Lesson Plans 87
Sample Projects 87
Sample Lesson Plans 96

eResources

The STEAM rubrics in this book are also available for free download on our website, so you can print them for classroom use. You can access these downloads by visiting the book product page on our website: www.routledge.com/9781138586635. Then click on the tab that reads "eResources" and select the file(s) you need. The file(s) will download directly to your computer.

Meet the Authors

Billy Krakower is a nationally recognized author. He has spoken at various national and regional events including the Empower18, National Principal's Conference 2017, Empower17, ASCD16, ISTE 2015, ISTE2014, New Jersey Association of School Administrators, Techspo, New Jersey Association of Educational Technology Annual Conference, Edscape, NJEA, Teacher Conference, among others.

Billy is also one of the co-moderators of #satchat on Twitter. Billy has co-written four other books, *Connecting Your Students with the World*, *Using Technology to Engage Students with Learning Disabilities*, *140 Twitter Tips for Educators*, and *Hacking Google for Education*. He can be found at www.billykrakower.com and followed on Twitter @wkrakower.

Meredith Martin is a Certified Google for Education Innovator and Trainer. She was a 2015 Bammy Awards nominee and frequently presents at conferences such as ISTE. She is founder of techforteachers.com and can be followed on Twitter @geekyteach.

Preface

Why the book *Getting Started with STEAM: Practical Strategies for the K–8 Classroom*? Both Meredith and Billy have a passion for learning about STEAM and teaching STEAM. They are both educators who look for ways to bring the components into their classroom. The idea of this book came to Meredith and Billy a few years ago and they have slowly been working out all the details until they finally decided to go to a publisher to see if there was interest.

Our belief is that STEAM can easily be taught, with the right guidance. There are so many different philosophies out there on the way in which to teach STEAM and there may not be one right way. We developed this book to be used as a guide to give teachers a starting point. We share examples of what has worked in our classrooms and ways in which you can begin. We include stories from members of our professional learning network (PLN), as well as their beliefs or views of STEAM or makerspace. We believe that although these terms are similar, there are differences between both STEAM and a makerspace; however, they both can exist in a school district.

Billy and Meredith believe one of the best resources out there is Twitter and have created a Twitter hashtag which you can use to share resources you might find useful and to continue your learning after you put this practical guide down; please follow #GSwSTEAM. This book is just a starting out point in the world of STEAM and we hope you continue to learn and share after you finish this book.

1

The What and Why of STEAM

The Jargon Jungle: Makers, STEM, and STEAM – What's the Difference?

The world of STEAM and making has exploded onto the educational scene in the past year. It seems that everywhere you turn, you are hearing about some form of making being implemented in schools. The terms STEM, STEAM, STREAM, makerspaces, FabLabs, Hackerspaces, MakerEd, Design Thinking, and more are bandied about in casual conversation but can be very confusing to those new to the movement. Billy and Meredith believe that many of these terms can be blended together. We will take a look at those terms in more detail shortly.

First, some background about what we have done, our philosophies with STEAM, and why sometimes STEAM can be blended with other terminology. Billy and Meredith both have experience in blending both STEAM and making in their respective roles in education, and are constantly developing new ways to combine these two types of hands-on education. Billy has worked to develop STEAM periods in his school and is currently working on developing STEAM during indoor recess. Meredith has developed a full-blown STEAM Lab for one school, and is currently developing a Technology and Makerspace program for the project-based learning school she currently teaches at. She also consults with schools and districts on how to develop and implement STEAM and maker programs in their own buildings.

Getting started blending STEAM and Making in education can seem intimidating and expensive. Billy and Meredith are aware of the funding issues facing most schools, and believe in finding the most cost-effective ways of incorporating STEAM/Making into schools. It is not only possible but easy to create a blended STEAM and Making program with very little financial expenditure.

Before we dive into the whys and hows of getting started with STEAM and Making, it's important to understand what those two terms mean, and the definitions of several related terms you may hear used in conjunction with them. The terms listed in the rest of this chapter will give you more of a background into what the terminology is and the ways in which we define these words.

STEM

STEM stands for Science, Technology, Engineering, and Math. While these subjects are often taught in schools, the philosophy behind STEM is integrating these subjects in meaningful ways instead of teaching them in isolated classes. STEM is a way of showing students how these core topics are interconnected to each other in the real world. STEM lessons and labs tend to be more structured than the more interest-driven makerspaces.

STEAM

STEAM stands for Science, Technology, Engineering, Arts and Math. The philosophy behind STEAM is integrating the arts into these subjects in a creative way. The arts is not just limited to the creative arts (drawing, painting, sculptures, 3D printing, music) but can include language arts as well. STEAM leads students to apply design and the arts as part of problem-solving. STEAM also encourages students to explore their creativity as part of their learning.

STREAM

STREAM is a newer iteration of STEAM. The R most often stands for either Research or wRiting. The philosophy behind STEAM is integrating research and/or writing into problem-solving. Research fits particularly well into many STEAM projects, particularly where students are asked to support their decisions as part of a project or activity. Writing, of course, is a necessary skill across all disciplines and parts of a project, from writing a

Figure 1.1 STEM, STEAM, and STREAM

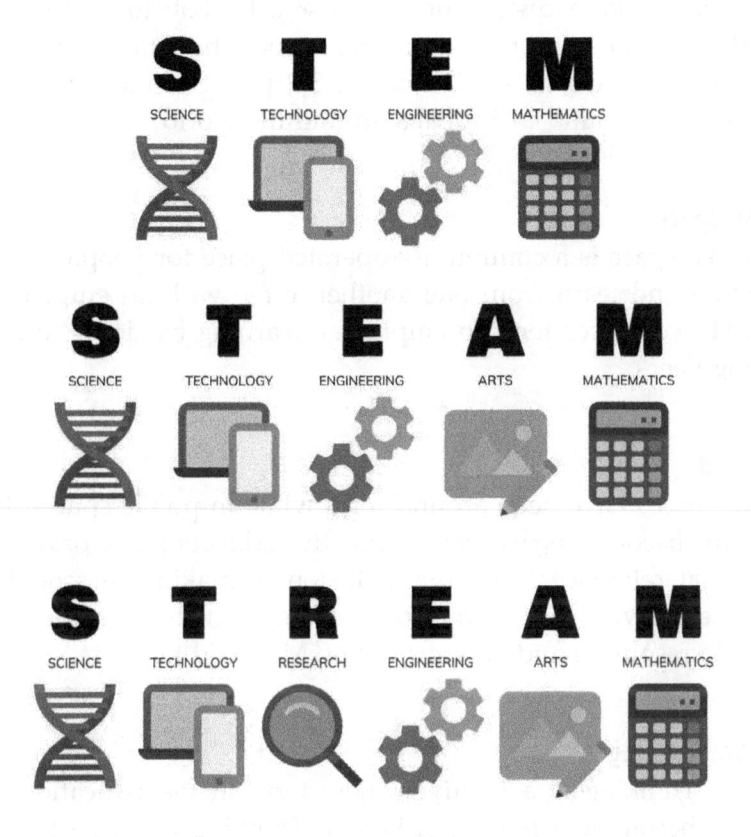

STEM
SCIENCE   TECHNOLOGY   ENGINEERING   MATHEMATICS

STEAM
SCIENCE   TECHNOLOGY   ENGINEERING   ARTS   MATHEMATICS

STREAM
SCIENCE   TECHNOLOGY   RESEARCH   ENGINEERING   ARTS   MATHEMATICS

proposal through recording data, all the way through to sharing a conclusion and presenting results (Figure 1.1).

Makerspaces
The term makerspace has many definitions and can be interpreted differently by each individual. The main idea behind a makerspace is that it is an OPEN area for students to explore and learn. Makerspaces tend to be more unstructured, and often have people working on widely varied types of projects. In schools, makerspaces are usually an area where students have more choice, and have the opportunity to explore their own interests and ideas.

FabLabs
A FabLab (short for fabrication laboratory) is a workshop area that can be used by members of the public for small-scale fabrication projects and

activities. People looking to create new products either for personal use or for limited sale or distribution can use a FabLab to access tools that have traditionally been restricted to mass-production factories and labs. Tools such as laser cutters, CNC routers, 3D printers, metalworking tools, and others can be found in FabLabs around the world.

Hackerspaces

A Hackerspace is a community-operated place for people to come together to tinker and learn from one another, often with an emphasis on technology. Hackerspaces tend to emphasize learning by doing and collaboration among peers.

MakerEd

Makerspaces have been around for a while in public spaces, but have only recently become incorporated into the educational world. MakerEd is a term that references both the inclusion of making in school subjects, but also the growing community of educators involved in the movement that provide resources and support fellow MakerEd teachers.

Design Thinking

Design Thinking is a relatively new term in the education world, but is rapidly becoming a hot topic. Design Thinking is a way to bring empathy into the classroom by teaching students to use their STEM and Making skills to meet the needs of others, instead of just themselves. Students often use Design Thinking to help solve real-world problems for their communities and the wider world.

These are the terms that are currently being used by many educators who are in the K–12 classroom. As you can see from the definitions above, there tends to be a lot of overlap between terms and many people use them interchangeably. The two main terms we are focusing on in this book are STEAM and Making. We believe that these terms are most applicable in an educational setting, and can be blended with one another with great results.

> **Maker is a mindset, more than it is a space. By Amanda Kavanagh**
> *What?* An area, space, place or concept where materials are available to be used for a creative process. This can include low-tech material such as paper-towel rolls, rubber bands, popsicle sticks, duct tape, paper and glue and/or 3D

printers, iPads, Chromebooks, Ozobots, Sphero, Raspberry Pi, Little Bits, or other high-tech devices.

Where? A makerspace can be anywhere. The corner of a classroom, the center of a classroom, within a Library Media Center, a stand-alone room designed for this purpose, or even a portable maker cart that can be moved from room to room. *It can also be a way of thinking in a classroom where any materials are fair game and the teacher lets the students use the design process to construct a representation of their knowledge.*

What happens in a makerspace? Depends on the grade level, materials and individuals occupying the space. Everything from self-directed creations to curriculum-aligned projects.

Our Approach (Hewlett-Woodmere Public Schools):

- Start with library media specialists (LMS) in the library in three buildings and a stand-alone makerspace in one of the buildings.

- Provide time for the LMS to write curriculum with assistance and support from the building principals and director of technology. Approximately 20% of the Library curriculum is dedicated to Technology Education (digital citizenship, maker, engineering, digital design, coding).

- This led to the creation of a roadmap to guide the LMS through the first year. A list of items that we needed to get this off the ground was made and purchased. This included:

    o Green screen
    o iPads
    o Chromebooks
    o 3D Printer
    o Bloxels
    o Code and Go Mouse (early elementary)
    o Doodle Pens
    o Osmo Kits
    o Ozobots (early elementary)
    o Sphero Robots (higher elementary grades)
    o Little Bits
    o Low-tech materials
    o Breakout EDU boxes.

> - The process has not looked the same in each building. Professional learning is ongoing for the LMS and they are transferring knowledge to the teachers in the buildings and working to make connections with the curriculum in conjunction with our Technology Integration Lead Teachers (TILTs).
>
> *How is a makerspace different and/or similar to a STEM/STEAM/Innovation Lab?*
>
> I wouldn't say that they are different or the same because each makerspace, even within one district, can be utilized differently. The main difference, from what I have seen, is who occupies this space and what the district's vision is for this type of learning. The most critical thing for Hewlett-Woodmere Public Schools (HWPS) was getting all of our stakeholders together to have a conversation about what this would look like in HWPS. What would this mean for our students and teachers? Although we started with our elementary buildings, our middle-school LMS has been bringing these concepts into her library for several years. We are now in the process of purchasing materials for our high school library. We are letting this grow naturally to meet the students and teachers where they are.

Now You Have the WHAT, Let's Find Out the WHY

Even more important than knowing what these terms mean is understanding why they have become such a strong force in the educational community. Before implementing any new program in a school or district, it's important to make sure that it has a strong pedagogical reason for being added. There are many powerful reasons for starting a MakerEd and STEAM program for your students. One reason it is important development these programs in our education system is because these will potential job fields for students to go into in the future. According to the United States Department of Commerce – Economic and Statistic Administration:

> Employment in STEM occupations grew much faster than employment in non-STEM occupations over the last decade (24.4 percent versus 4.0 percent, respectively), and STEM occupations are projected to grow by 8.9 percent from 2014 to 2024, compared to 6.4 percent growth for non- STEM occupations.[1]

If these will be the potential jobs for our students, we should be teaching our students these skills at an early age and exposing them to the different mindset of thinking in STEM-related fields. What is even more interesting is that "In 2015, there were 9.0 million STEM workers in the United States. About 6.1 percent of all workers are in STEM occupations, up from 5.5 percent just five years earlier.[2]" These numbers show why we need to make sure we start to develop a STEM program in our schools. The question or the argument can be: then why do we need to discuss STEAM or STREAM? In our view, making sure you add the "A" into STEM is important to help students have a better understanding of how all the subject areas tie in together.

Why add "A" in STEM
Often we discuss what the A in STEAM stands for, and the response is the arts. Let's make that arts–not just the creative arts but creative writing and the PERFORMING arts as well.

There is a buzz in schools around the Science, Technology, Engineering, and Mathematics, or STEM. Schools across the country are adopting or finding ways to incorporate STEM into children's school days. Often there is a discussion about whether or not it should be STEM or as some people call it, STEAM (Science, Technology, Engineering, Art and Mathematics). What the difference is often comes down to the ways in which people will interpret the meaning behind it. In my mind, the A is important to add to the discussion when we are talking about STEM. It makes sense to add the A; from this educator's standpoint you want students to become creative when designing. Having the A expands the idea of STEM into STEAM and allows for a more rounded student learning experience. Students are often very engaged in learning about STEAM and learning valuable skills such as collaborations, teamwork, and critical thinking. These skills are essential for students to learn, as they are necessary life skills to have and they help develop relationships skills in education life.

However, there is a common misunderstanding where people assume the A only stands for creative arts, which include drawing, painting, paper and fabric making to name a few. Stop and think for a second – why can't we make the argument that the A also stands for literary or performing arts? What if we looked at fairy tales and found ways in which we can incorporate STEM into those? Then we can consider it to be STEAM. Let's take a look at a classic fairy tale, "The Three Little Pigs." Start off by reading the story of "The Three Little Pigs." There are many different version of the story; it doesn't matter which interpretation of the story you find, but you want to make sure the story discusses the materials the pigs use to build their houses. After reading the story, your students can build a house out of straws, wood (popsicles sticks) and brick (index cards). You can use a big box-fan as the wolf to test out the students' houses and see if they stand up to the Big Bad Wolf. For more information about this lesson, visit Chapter 4 as we explore more about incorporating the arts and literacy into STEAM.

While the "doing" of STEM/STEAM work is key, the need to link it back to relevant learning is still paramount. That's why connecting to fairy tales is so powerful for younger learners.

Technology Is Not Just Computers

In our current society, when people think about technology they think of a computer or a tablet. Technology, however, is more than just those few devices. Technology is everywhere and part of our everyday life. When it comes down to the school setting, technology is forever changing the ways in which we teach, learn and communicate. Computers have changed the way we do this but students are now learning how to code robots, create 3D designs on the computer and 3D-print those designs.

Coding is a huge topic in education. It has become more popular with the launch of Computer Science Week (https://csedweek.org/). More and more schools are looking for ways to include programming as part of their computer science curriculum. Coding is often thought of as a higher-level skill, more suitable for high school and older students, but the truth is that the underlying concepts of programming are accessible to ALL levels, even pre-school and kindergarten! Programming can be taught to any grade level, provided you keep it appropriate for their age and development. You don't even need a computer to get started teaching the key concepts of coding. In Meredith's kindergarten class, students begin their introduction to coding with several offline activities. A perennial favorite (and not just for little kids!) is human programming. Students pair up, with one being the program and the other being the programmer. The program has to navigate to a predetermined spot in the room by following the directions of the programmer student … exactly. This leads to lots of giggles in the beginning when the novice programmers tell their programs to "go forward" and the human program continues walking right into object in the room because the programmer was not specific enough. The programmers quickly learn to be more specific and concise in their instruction, moving from commands like "go forward" to "walk ten steps forward, turn ninety degrees right, walk five steps forward". It's a fun and easy way to introduce concepts such as logic, algorithms, and debugging. When five year olds are excitedly explaining to the principal how they "debugged their algorithms" today, you know it's been a successful lesson. There are many other "unplugged" coding activities, including making binary bracelets and board games such as Robot Turtles and Code Master.

3D design is a way not only to incorporate the T in STEAM but also the A, as students are becoming artists using a different platform. It is often assumed that you need 3D printers in order to teach 3D design, but nothing could be further from the truth. While you certainly CAN design things to be 3D printed using a variety of websites and apps, you don't need any of that to successfully teach 3D design. Modeling is a great way to learn about and show understanding of concepts in many different disciplines. Long before 3D printers were available, students and teachers were creating models and prototypes in classrooms. Go back to basics! Who needs a pricey 3D printer when you can design with clay or construction paper? Why not find ways to reuse everyday items in models? Sometimes low-tech is the way to go.

There are many different types of robots that students can use today, and while some require a computer, tablet, or smartphone to program, not all of them do. One robot that is easy to use and does not require a computer to use, and is a great add to a STEAM program is an Ozobot (https://ozobot.com/) Ozobots are robots that follow simple line instructions and can be used with just markers to have them follow commands. These are a great introduction to robots and programming for younger kids. They can easily learn the color codes used to program the robots and complete a variety of challenges with them.

Circuits are another great tech tool that can be taught without the need for computers or tablets. For beginners, creating simple circuits with LEDs, copper tape, and coin cell batteries is both easy and fun. Students can build up from there to learn about different types of circuits and switches. Chibitronics (https://chibitronics.com/) makes a variety of circuit stickers that students can use to create their own interactive art. From the basics of paper circuits, students can move up to more complex and interactive circuits. Lilypad sewable electronics (https://www.sparkfun.com/lilypad_sewable_electronics) are another great way to teach students about circuits, and allow them to create amazing interactive wearables along the way. A favorite circuit activity for both Meredith and Billy is mini lightsabers made to celebrate Star Wars Day. (See sample lessons in the appendix.)

As we said, don't fall into the habit of thinking technology is limited to computers and tablets. Merriam-Webster defines technology, in part, as:

"the practical application of knowledge especially in a particular area."[3] Nowhere in the definition does it mention computers at all! Break the habit, and start looking for new ways to apply knowledge in your areas of education.

Reflection Questions

- What do you view as the difference between STEM, STEAM, or STREAM? Do you think it matters?
- Think about technology that you currently have available. How can you incorporate what you already have into a STEAM program?
- Why is adding the A in STEAM important? How does it affect your students?

Notes

1. Esa.doc.gov. (2017). *STEM Jobs: 2017 Update | Economics & Statistics Administration*. [online] Available at: www.esa.doc.gov/reports/stem-jobs-2017-update. Accessed 26 Dec. 2017.
2. Esa.doc.gov. (2017). *STEM Jobs: 2017 Update | Economics & Statistics Administration*. [online] Available at: www.esa.doc.gov/reports/stem-jobs-2017-update [Accessed 26 Dec. 2017].
3. "Technology | Definition of Technology by Merriam-Webster." www.merriam-webster.com/dictionary/technology. Accessed 14 Jan. 2018.

2

Planning Your STEAM Space

Introduction

In Chapter 1, we gave a brief overview of the differences between STEAM and makerspaces. The key difference between the two is usually in the amount of pre-planning and structure that go into activities, although there can also be a significant amount of crossover between the two.

One thing that STEAM spaces and traditional makerspaces have in common is that there is no "one right way" to design them. Both types of spaces are inherently flexible and can adapt to many different locations and situations. Have a dedicated room for your space? Awesome! Want to integrate STEAM into all of the classrooms instead of having a separate space? No problem. Don't have dedicated space in the building or a classroom? Easy solutions abound! Let's take a look at what some of these spaces look like, and start planning how to develop your own.

What Does a Dedicated Space Look Like?

Space is often at a premium in schools, so it can be difficult to wrangle a dedicated room or space for STEAM. If you have an entire room at your disposal, congratulations! The hard work is already done. Other schools have gotten creative with space for their STEAM labs, and incorporated them into existing rooms. The Media Center and Computer Lab are most often the rooms tapped to host a STEAM or makerspace.

In Meredith's original school, she began a campaign to convert the computer lab into a STEAM space when she learned that students would be going 1:1 with Chromebooks the following year. After many discussions with administration, she was able to get the go-ahead to convert the old, outdated lab into a STEAM lab. Out went the rows of computer desks that had been built into the floor. In came new electrical outlets around the perimeter, flexible seating arrangements, and extra storage. Add in a new paint job and some simple supplies, and the new STEAM lab was ready to launch!

Every STEAM space has its own unique look and personality based on the needs of the students and the use of the space. A STEAM lab for lower-elementary students is going to look different than one designed for middle- or high-school students. Before beginning to design your space, it's important to do some planning about how the space will be used. Think about what types of projects you will be using the space for. If you are planning on using lots of tech and tools, it is important to consider things like power and workspace. Doing a lot of messy stuff? A sink in the room is a definite plus! What types of materials will you be needing to store? Do you have space to keep projects-in-progress safe and organized? Let's break this down a bit:

Seating

This is a big consideration. Not only do you have to consider the age and size of your students—kindergarten kids won't do well with tables designed for high schoolers, and vice versa!—but also the types of work you will be doing. If you're planning on using a lot of tools or potentially caustic materials, a heavy-duty worktop such as a shop table may be best. If you're using less heavy-duty materials, a regular tabletop works just fine.

Flexible seating is recommended as much as possible. Meredith's favorite furniture in her STEAM lab were the diamond-shaped tables that could be combined in a variety of configurations. When one or two students were working on a project, they could pull one of the tables out to make a personal workspace. For groups of three or more, three tables could be combined into a pod that could fit six or more team members. For whole class activities or presentations, the tables could be arranged into larger pods, a horseshoe shape, or other large group setup, very easily. Being able to rearrange the furniture to meet the different needs of various projects is incredibly useful.

Power

Power is another big consideration for a STEAM or makerspace. This is true whether or not you are planning lots of high-tech lessons or not. If you are using power tools, electronics, and computers, it seems obvious that you want lots of accessible power. What many people don't think about is how useful these power ports are in a low-tech lab as well. One of the favorite low-tech tools that requires power in Meredith's classrooms is hot glue guns! These little three-dollar tools are useful for everything from arts projects, to prototyping, to putting the finishing touches on a presentation. There would often be ten glue guns at use in various parts of the classroom at any time during a project.Other common items used in the lab that required power ranged from blenders, to a hot water kettle, to hair dryers! You'd be surprised how many everyday powered items you can find use for in a STEAM lab. Make sure you have good access to power, whether it's from wall outlets, ceiling drops, or even the old standby of power strips. (Extension cords are also worth their weight in gold!)

Storage

Storage is hugely important. STEAM and maker labs give teachers a chance to really give in to our natural hoarding tendencies. You never know what materials and supplies may end up useful in a project. Meredith's spaces always had several "donation stations" available for students, families, and other teachers to drop off items from paper towel tubes to old electronics, and everything in between. Lack of storage has several downsides. It can make finding needed supplies more difficult and time consuming, it can look messy, making it a turn-off to administrators and other visitors, and more importantly it can also become a safety hazard. Keep in mind that not only do you need storage for supplies, but also for projects-in-progress!Get creative with your storage. If your room has built-in cabinets and closets, you've won the lottery! If not, it's time to stretch your teacher's foraging muscles. Bookcases and old cabinets or cubbies can be excellent storage units. Many schools have a storage or custodial room where unused furniture is being stored. Time to go spelunking! Ask around to see if fellow teachers have items they want to get out of their classroom. Many times teachers are stuck with a piece of unwanted furniture simply because there is no other place to store it. The end and beginning of the school year are the best times to ask, because many people are cleaning up or reorganizing their classrooms then.

Think beyond furniture. How are you going to store and organize supplies, particularly smaller ones? Rubbermaid bins are excellent for storing larger items, and smaller plastic containers are great for items like glue guns, markers, tape, and more. Recycle plastic jars for tiny loose items such as beads, sewing tools, toothpicks, or LEDs.

Once you have the physical storage, don't forget to keep it organized. Create a labeling system that works for you, and make sure the students and other teachers are familiar with it. Having supplies clearly labeled and organized not only makes the room look more appealing, but also saves a lot of time when prepping for a lesson or a project. This can seem like a huge project if you have a ton of supplies, but this is a great chance to get the students involved. Have them help label, organize, and decide where things go. This has two benefits – first, it saves you time and energy. Second, it gives students some ownership in the space.

Other Considerations
Seating, power, and storage are the Big Three when considering a dedicated STEAM space, but there are lots of other things that can be pulled in to make your space even better. Here are a few suggestions:

1. **Writable table tops** – These are amazing. You can turn any surface into a whiteboard in a few simple steps. Using either whiteboard contact paper or whiteboard paint, student tables can quickly be turned into spaces to sketch, write, and share ideas.
2. **Whiteboard walls** – Why stop at tabletops? A whole wall coated in whiteboard paint gives students the chance to be creative and share their thinking on a large scale. Can't paint the wall? Why not buy (or better yet, MAKE!) some portable whiteboards on wheels that can be moved around the room and used during small group work? White showerboard from a hardware store such as Lowes or Home Depot is an inexpensive way to make custom whiteboards!
3. **Green screen** – Turn part of your space into a film studio. There are a ton of inexpensive green screen kits available at places like Amazon; grab a gallon of Green Screen paint and cover a wall; or even use a green table cover from the dollar store to make a creative space to film.
4. **Sinks** – The importance of a sink in or near a STEAM lab cannot be overestimated. Whether you are using water as part of a project on density and buoyancy or cleaning up after a project that incorporated cornstarch and food coloring, a sink is incredibly useful.

Now that you have an overview of what a dedicated space needs, start thinking about your own space. What parts do you already have? What do you need? How can you put it all together? Be creative, and make it your own!

What Does STEAM Look Like Integrated into Classrooms?

An alternative to having a dedicated space for STEAM is integrating it into the classrooms. One of the benefits of integrating STEAM into a classroom is that it makes it become part of students' everyday learning, not just something special that they do once in a while or that they go to a special space to do.

The first step to integrating this into your classroom is to take a look at your curriculum and find the best places where it can be incorporated. You don't necessarily need to have a STEAM activity for every lesson, but you should pick the lessons and activities where it would best fit. This can be easy when you're looking at a subject such as science, but there are many ways to incorporate STEAM into other areas of the curriculum as well.

Let's start by taking a look at a simple science lesson. In this scenario the students are studying fossils. Why not incorporate a simple STEAM lab where in addition to learning the facts, they also have a chance to create their own fossils. This can be done very simply with plaster of Paris and some clay or playdough. Students can use small items such as shells, rocks or plastic toys to make an impression in the clay or playdough, and then add plaster of Paris to make casts of the mold just like real scientists do when they find fossils in the wild.

Another fun science example is learning about crystals. Students can use a simple borax and water solution to learn about how crystals form and also about terms such as "solution" and "supersaturation". Once they've created their crystals it's a great chance to look at them under a magnifying glass or microscope and study the different shapes that they make. Try making crystals with different materials. Does it change the structure of the crystal? Do different types of materials create different kinds of crystals? Activities like this can also include a lot of math such as studying volume, ratios, and various measurements.

In an example from Meredith's school, a math class needed to learn area, perimeter, and volume. They could have just done worksheets and drills, but instead they decided to find another way to do it. The students had recently received a large shipment of books as part of a previous project and now they needed a way to store the books in the classroom. Why not incorporate the skills of calculating area, perimeter, and volume as part of a project to find ways to store these books? Students then learned about area, perimeter, and volume as they designed bookcases to hold the books that they had in their classrooms. In addition to just learning the math skills, they also learned about design sketching and drawing, and designed a simple tool to help them create the bookcases. During the course of this project, high-school students from the local Workshop School came in to help students with their project and to judge the final designs. The winning designs were chosen, and then the students built the physical bookcases. Now every classroom in the building has a bookcase design by students from that math class. Those students never did a worksheet or drill, but they will never forget the skills and concepts of area, perimeter, and volume.

There are many great ways to add STEAM into your everyday classroom lessons. It just requires some investment of time and creativity to sit down and find the best areas of the curriculum to add it to. Don't try to force it into everything, but instead find where it fit naturally.

Other Spaces and Ways to Incorporate STEAM

A dedicated space, or being integrated into the classrooms, are two big ways to incorporate STEAM into your school, but not all schools or situations make this possible. How can you find ways to create a STEAM space when you are lacking in ... space? Thankfully, there are ways you can infuse STEAM into your school and curriculum even when you don't have a lot of space to dedicate to it. Here are some examples:

1. **STEAM boxes** – In Meredith's first school, she was splitting her time between two buildings. When she wasn't in her STEAM lab, she was in a lower-elementary building, teaching technology. The question became how to get other teachers involved in adding STEAM lessons to their classes when she was out of the building? The solution? STEAM boxes! Empty Xerox boxes were repurposed to hold mini STEAM labs. Each box became home to a set of supplies needed for a simple activity such as the Marshmallow Challenge, hovercraft, or catapults. There were enough materials in each box for one class to complete the activity, along with printed guidelines for the teachers, and any handouts needed for the students. Teachers did not need any prior experience with the lab, they simply needed to follow the instructions included in the box. The only "work" they had to do was to let Meredith know when they used a box so it could be restocked with any consumables that had

been used. These easy, engaging, and educational activities made it easy for any classroom teacher to pick up a box and get started with a STEAM lab.

2. **STEAM at recess** – These STEAM boxes were an offshoot of Meredith's STEAM boxes. Several members from a school district approached Meredith at a conference with questions on how to incorporate STEAM and Making in a school with limited space. During the conversation, it was mentioned how rowdy indoor recess could get. This was the perfect opportunity to incorporate STEAM during recess. The school set up several STEAM and maker boxes that were kept in the lunchroom, and on inclement weather days, the tables that were well behaved had their choice of projects to work on from the boxes. When they touched base later on, the school had already seen a decrease in behavior problems during indoor recess times as students were excited at the chance to get their hands on one of the boxes and start learning and creating!

At Billy's school he has developed a STEAM recess plan: he came up with the idea and plan after talking with Meredith at EdcampNJ. Due to a lack of funding, he thought about applying for an Edcamp Impact Grant. Having attended an Edcamp, he could take what he learned at the Edcamp and apply for funding through the Edcamp organization. Before coming up with a set plan for indoor recess, Billy had a conversation with his principal, Mrs. Sharon Tomback, who was highly supportive of the idea and made several suggestions about the project, including getting the student input first before purchasing materials. The first step was to have a meeting with each grade level to show them the different items that we could purchase, gauge their interest level, and see what suggestions they might have. One important key here was getting all groups involved in this decisions as one wants to make sure that one has student interest.

Collaboration was important in developing this plan, as Billy is not the only one who has recess duty; the physical education teacher Mr. Gaetano Pompante also had duty and would be working closely with the students on the implementation of the project. Billy wrote the grant and did receive funding from the Edcamp organization for the indoor recess plan. However, a solid plan needed to be put in place in order for chaos not to ensue. The items that were purchased with the grant were K'nexes, Keva Planks, some storage containers, binders and sheet protectors. Some of the items were purchased in order to keep everything organized and smoothly run.

Billy and Gaetano met several times during the winter and spring months to discuss the different activities the students will be participating in and developed group parameters for the students to follow. Gaetano shared with Billy rules that he has been developing for physical education and, with a little tweaking, they developed the roles for indoor recess and Billy even used the roles for his STEAM class. These roles include: The Facilitator, The Recorder, The Summarizer, The Timekeeper, The Reflector, and The Equipment Manager. We will explore these roles in more depth in Chapter 4.

We developed a binder system that includes models and activities for two of the items we purchased which are K'nex and Keva Planks. These binders are used by the students when they are working with these materials. When students are working with other materials such as the Ready, Set, Design! materials, they are given a paper bag or plastic box to keep the materials organized. Keep in mind that we are always revisiting indoor recess and making changes to improve the flow and activities.

3. **Hallway STEAM** – Glenn Robbins, then a principal and now a superintendent in New Jersey, had an amazing idea. He took an old computer that had been removed from a classroom because it was old and slow, and disassembled it down to its base components. The box of parts was placed on a table in the hallway, along with a challenge to the students to see if they could get it assembled and running again. Not only did the students complete the challenge, but Glenn soon had a delegation of students approach him to ask if he could add a second disassembled computer to the challenge so that they could compete to see if the boys or girls could assemble it faster.

4. **Mystery bags** – A fun and simple way to add some STEAM to a classroom or lesson is by setting up mystery bags. These are simply brown sandwich bags filled with a variety of everyday materials and a card with a simple scenario or challenge. For example, a bag may contain some popsicle sticks, some dental floss, a spool, a plastic spoon, two Lego minifigs, a paper cup, and some paper clips. The scenario may be that one minifig has fallen off a cliff, and you are the rescue squad that has to design a way to get them safely back up to the top for medical treatment. Get creative and have fun!

5. **Creative learning** – As told by Marissa Urso, Library Media Specialist, Goosehill Primary (K-1), Cold Spring Harbor School District, NY.

   I've started working this year in a creative learning lab, which is a space dedicated to bring STEM to our boys and girls teaching them to explore, experiment, make, create, and fail-forward. My students learn in their own way and time. They are better able to facilitate and collaborate when we make time and space for STEM integration into our curriculum.

   In the K-1 buildings as well as the 2–6 buildings in our district, we were able to renovate a room dedicated to STEM. However, STEM doesn't need a separate room in order to happen, but an open mindset that it isn't about teacher talk but as much about education that is student-driven. In some of our Creative Learning Labs, we have whiteboards, flexible seating, couches, a makerspace, a 3D printer and a soundproof room for student recording.

   We focus on "genius hour" in our STEM environments because it is about giving students the ownership of their learning—they can research their own projects, have space to collaborate, and then the teachers can continue the conversation back in their classrooms. At the K-1 level, I co-teach with teachers, introduce STEM tools, give teachers resources and guide them in this new concept of learning so that students have more freedom regarding content and an opportunity for inquiry-based learning. Currently, our students are working on building a shade to keep an ice-cube from melting where they have to research, measure, build and test, test, test!

   Our Creative Learning Lab is really about working together and introducing new tools in a fun and engaging way as we teach content in an innovative manner. It is a space where students learn how to overcome struggle and the most important aspect is that elements of STEM can happen anywhere!

Making and STEAM, a Perfect Combination

Although this chapter focuses mostly on creating a space for STEAM, much of the same things hold true when creating a makerspace. The main difference between a STEAM and a makerspace is, as we mentioned earlier, the amount of structure. The same things that make a STEAM space so awesome – flexible seating, lots of power, storage and organization – are also things that work well in a makerspace. Don't forget, that your space can combine aspects of both. It does not have to be one or the other, but could be used as a STEAM lab one day, and a more open-ended makerspace on another.

Reflection Questions

You've now read about several ways to set up a STEAM program, from large to small.

- What will your STEAM program look like?
- Does one of the styles listed in this chapter fit your needs perfectly, or would a combination of several styles work better for you?

3

Stocking Your Space
What Supplies Do You Need?

Now that you have your space, the fun begins. It's time to start stocking it. Every space should include the basics such as scissors, pencils, paper, glue, and tape. Beyond those basics, the possibilities are endless. There are many ways to stock your STEAM space, but the first step is to decide what types of projects and activities you're going to be doing in it so that you know what types of materials you need to get. These will vary from space to space, but in this chapter we'll cover some of the basics from the super-low-tech to the super-high-tech and everything in between.

Don't Break the Bank: Dollar Store STEAM Supplies

A common misconception about STEAM spaces is that they need to be high-tech and include a lot of expensive tools and materials. Nothing could be further from the truth. Many STEAM spaces can be stocked simply with everyday items, recyclable materials, and items from the dollar store (see Table 3.1). While having high-end, expensive equipment can be awesome, it's not the be-all and end-all of a STEAM program. In fact, many times having lower-tech, inexpensive materials can make a STEAM space even better for your students. Using low-cost or recyclable materials makes it easier for them to duplicate or expand upon projects you do in the lab at home on their own time. It's much

Table 3.1 A starter list of dollar store and recyclable items that can be invaluable in a STEAM program

From the Dollar Store	Recyclables
◆ Coffee filters ◆ Straws ◆ Toothpicks ◆ Rubber bands ◆ Index cards ◆ Q-tips ◆ Popsicle sticks ◆ Cupcake liners ◆ Masking tape ◆ Playing cards ◆ Pipe cleaners ◆ Mop bucket ◆ Paper plates ◆ Plastic silverware ◆ Plastic bins ◆ Magnets ◆ Duct tape ◆ Scotch tape ◆ Cotton balls ◆ Plastic baggies ◆ Plastic cups ◆ Felt ◆ Lunch bags ◆ String ◆ Dental floss ◆ Flashlights ◆ Envelopes ◆ Coffee stirrers ◆ Paper clips ◆ Foam boards ◆ Poster board ◆ Marshmallows (regular and mini) ◆ Gumdrops ◆ Spaghetti (uncooked) ◆ Balloons ◆ Battery operated toothbrushes ◆ Pool noodles	◆ Toilet paper tubes ◆ Paper towel tubes ◆ Shoeboxes ◆ Plastic jars & containers ◆ Legos or other engineering toys ◆ Egg cartons ◆ Old CDs/DVDs ◆ CD cases ◆ Empty soda bottles ◆ Old electronics (solar devices especially) ◆ Cardboard ◆ Bottle and jar caps ◆ Electronic or mechanical toys ◆ Old, clean clothing ◆ Fabric scraps ◆ Thread and spools ◆ Yarn scraps ◆ Matchbox cars

easier for a student to ask his/her parents for $5 to spend at the local dollar store than it is for the student to ask for $500 to purchase a 3D printer.

You can make a wide variety of projects and labs with these everyday materials and dollar store items. For example, using simply marshmallows and uncooked spaghetti your students can compete in the marshmallow tower challenge. Battery-operated toothbrushes provide simple motors that can be used to create robots that move via vibrations. Popsicle sticks, rubber bands, a plastic spoon, and a marshmallow can become a catapult. Old electronics and mechanical toys can be disassembled and scavenged for parts that can be used in other projects, or they can be modified as part of a larger project. One of the best things about dollar stores is that their stock is always changing, so you never know what you're going to find each time you walk in. Many awesome projects have been created simply from a walk through a dollar store checking out all of the awesome materials and considering their potential.

Inexpensive Electronics

Electronics can be a fun and educational addition to any STEAM program. The variety of electronic tools and parts available today mean there is something for every budget and every skill level. There are innumerable ways to include electronics in your curriculum even if you have never used them before.

A simple way to get started is with LEDs, copper tape, and coin cell batteries. These three inexpensive, easy-to-get items open up a whole world of learning and engagement. Students can quickly learn about electricity and circuits while making lightup paper cards and projects.

As mentioned earlier, one of Meredith's favorite activities to introduce simple circuits is by creating mini lightsabers on Star Wars Day (May 4th). This project is always a big hit with kids and grownups alike. All you need are some plastic straws in different colors (the larger milkshake straws work best), LEDs, coin cell batteries, and some colorful duct tape or electrical tape. Students learn how to create a simple circuit and learn about positive and negative poles while taping an LED onto a coin cell battery to make it light up. The LED is then slid into a colored straw to make the saber blade, while more tape is used to attach the battery to the straw to create the hilt (Figure 3.1).

From this simple activity, students can branch out into creating more complex circuits with copper tape and other conductive materials. Squishy Circuits – creating 3D objects that incorporate a variety of circuits using conductive and insulative play-dough – are another way to spark interest in electronics and circuits. You can purchase Squishy Circuit kits online, or use your own batteries, LEDs, motors, and more to create your own kit. The recipes for both types of dough are freely available online.

Another great way to introduce circuits and electronics is with sewable circuits. Create light-up or interactive plushies, accessories, clothes, and more with just LEDs, batteries, and some conductive thread. You can keep it simple, or use LilyPad sewable circuit kits for more complex creations.

Figure 3.1 Cathy Cheo-Issacs learning how to make LED coin cell light sabers at EdcampNJ 2015

The MakeyMakey is a great way to move from basic circuits into the realm of physical computing. This small, inexpensive circuit board connects to a computer and lets you turn almost any item into a controller. Play Pac-Man using graphite sketches on a piece of paper, or turn your students into a human synth. This simple tool has endless possibilities in the classroom.

Meredith's current favorite electronic tool is the BBC Micro:bit. You can get this amazing little circuit board for $15. Its built-in LED and sensors are completely programmable, and it has multiple physical connector pins that let you add in speakers, motors, external LEDs, and more. The Micro:bit is extremely scalable for all ages and skill levels. Beginners can program it with a simple drag and drop block language, while more experienced students can move into programming with Python or JavaScript. Best of all, its small size and portable nature mean it can be built into a variety of projects and presentations with ease.

The next steps up from tools like the MakeyMakey and the Micro:bit are Raspberry Pi computers and Arduino circuit boards. These are a little more complex than the previously mentioned beginner circuit boards, but are still easy enough for the beginner to pick up. The Raspberry Pi is an amazingly affordable computer that fits in the palm of your hand. It ranges in price from $5 to $35, and all you need is a monitor, mouse, and keyboard to attach it to. Arduinos are simple circuit boards, sensors, and components that can be used in conjunction with things like the Raspberry Pi to create more complex and customized electronics projects.

If you are looking to get started with some basic robotics but dread the cost of higher-end tools like Lego's Mindstorms, there are many entry-level robots to get started with. For younger students, the Ozobot is a tiny wheeled computer that is controlled by color codes. The modern generations of Ozobots are also codable using a drag and drop block language.

Sphero also makes some fun, easy to program robots that won't kill your budget. The original Sphero is a ball-shaped robot that can be controlled by an app or programmed in the drag and drop editor. Their newer Sphero Mini is about half the cost, and also easily programmable. They have a great educator section on their website complete with a teacher guide to getting started.

Another entry level robot is the Finch. This adorable little robot is deceptively powerful. It can be programmed with a multitude of languages and includes a ton of great features. The Finch contains accelerometers, motors, a buzzer, light, temperature, and obstacle sensors, and even a pen mount for drawing! For $99 it is an excellent addition to any beginner robotics program.

A Well-stocked Toolkit

It's time to jump back from high-tech to low-tech again! Never underestimate the importance of a well-stocked traditional tool kit. Screwdrivers, hammers, pliers, wrenches, and other basic tools are indispensable in a STEAM space. Not only are these tools perfect for building and creating prototypes and projects, but they are also very useful when it comes to deconstructing as well. Students can use them to take apart small electronics and other items to scavenge for parts that can then be added to the supplies available for other projects.

Small power tools, such as hot glue guns and rotary tools, are also very useful in any type of STEAM or makerspace. Hot glue guns are one of the most popular items in Meredith's makerspace, and the rotary tools also get used on a regular basis. One thing to keep in mind when shopping for things like hot glue guns is, of course, safety. There are a variety of different ones on the market, and we recommend sticking with a low-temp glue gun. These can be purchased for about $3 each, and the low temperature means that although they may sting if a student touches the hot end or the melted glue, they won't cause any serious burns or injuries. Having proper safety year-round is also important. At the very least try to have inexpensive safety goggles and aprons available to students at all times. Nitrile gloves are also handy to have around when dealing with messy or caustic materials.

Keep an eye out for inexpensive larger power tools as well. Even if you only have one of each power tool that the teacher has access to, it can make a huge difference. When you are doing a lot of building and prototyping, having at least one power drill on hand can be a lifesaver. Some power tools can be expensive, so check second hand stores for used items, or ask in the community for donations. Meredith's favorite source for inexpensive tools – both power and hand tools – is Harbor Freight. They always have a great variety of inexpensive tools that you can use in your STEAM program.

There are also several smaller items that can be extremely useful in a steam toolkit. In addition to the larger tools and items, consider things like a small magnetic bowl. If you are disassembling computers or other small electronics, this bowl is indispensable When it comes to keeping you from losing small screws and other parts. With this in mind, a set of small screwdrivers is also very handy if you're working with electronics. Magnifying glasses can be very handy, and we also recommend having a pack of zip ties in the toolkit as well. Zip ties are extremely useful in many situations.

If you are doing any projects with cardboard, one of the best small tools you can add to your toolkit is a cardboard cutter. Using regular scissors, even large ones, on cardboard can be extremely frustrating and even painful for students. While box cutters and similar utility knives can be used, safety is a huge issue with these tools. We recommend a safety cardboard cutter, which can be purchased very inexpensively from places like Amazon. Meredith's space keeps a handful of Klever Kutter safety box cutters on hand for cardboard projects. These cutters are small, easy to use for hands both large and small, cut easily through most cardboard, and best of all they are designed to make it virtually impossible to cut yourself.

Let's Splurge a Little

The majority of our focus in this chapter has been on ways to keep costs down while stocking your STEAM space. It's always good to be able to stick within a budget, but every once in a while you have the opportunity to splurge. If you have a larger budget or come into a windfall of funds that you can use to purchase larger, more expensive items, we have some recommendations for you.

A purchase that can be a nice add to any space would be a few littleBit sets. Billy is a huge fan of littleBits and has written grants to stock his space along with being a littleBit Lead Educator where he was able to preview the littleBit coding kits before they were released to the general public. A few kits that work perfectly in the classroom are the Gizmos and Gadgets Kit ($199.95), the STEAM Kit ($299.95) and the Code Kit ($299.95). These kits are perfect for small group instruction where they can usually accommodate three to four students. If you can afford the kits they are are great addition to any STEAM space.

The saying is "Go Big or Go Home" – with that said, if you are looking to make a large purchase we would recommend purchasing some type of 3D printer. There are many of them on the market these days, and the price range is fairly large. You can get a 3D printer for anywhere from $200 up to several thousand dollars. Our recommendation is to stick with some of the more inexpensive printers. 3D printing is still extremely slow and having multiple printers makes it easier for you to print out multiple prototypes at one time. Given the choice between three or four $200 printers or one $3,000 printer we recommend going with multiple $200 printers every time.

Many times we are asked which 3D printers are the best for a STEAM space. As with most things, there's no one correct answer for everybody, but we do have some recommendations of printers that we have had good experiences with. Top of the list at the time of writing is the Monoprice 3D printer. At just over $200 for the MP Select Mini 3D printer, this device is a little workhorse. The ones we have seen in action churn out print after print with little setup and no errors. If you're looking for an easy-to-use, low-cost entry-level printer, this one gets full marks.

Another great entry-level printer is the Printrbot Simple Pro. Ranging from $600-$700, it's more pricey than the Monoprice, but delivers a larger print bed and more features. Other great starter printers include the Dremel Digilab and the Flashforge Dreamer. Meredith is partial to the Flashforge Dreamer, which prints in dual colors, can handle multiple types of filaments, and has a heated bed. It's a little more expensive than some of the others, though, at about $900. Flashforge does make less expensive printers, but the authors have not tested any of them yet.

The next big item on our list is a laser cutter. At this point in time, these are truly a splurge item. Most quality lasers start at six to seven thousand dollars each, and require some more intensive training and setup. If you can afford one, though, go for it!

Not ready for the extreme outlay of funds for a laser? Consider a die cutting machine instead. With the rise of scrapbookers and other home creators, die cut machines such as the Cricut Explore Air or Maker, or the Silhouette machine are much less expensive and can do many of the things a laser can do on a smaller scale. These modern cutting tools can handle materials from paper, to cardstock, to vinyl, to leather, and even to chipboard with some models. If you're looking for a way to start some simple manufacturing projects with your students for under $250, these machines may be a good start.

Grants, Donations, and Other Ways to Stock Your Space

There are many different grants and ways in which to get donations in order to stock your space. Billy has received a few grants – he has been the recipient of an ASCD Grant and an Edcamp Impact grant. The best news if you have ever attend an Edcamp you can apply for an Edcamp Impact grant, for more information visit: www.edcamp.org/impact-grant. Billy talked about the project he did with his Edcamp Impact grant in Chapter 1 with his indoor recess plan.

Donors Choose is a well-known source of materials and supplies for teachers. Simply sign up on their website, create a project, and select the items you need from a variety of vendors. Donors from around the world can view and help fund projects on the site. There are often donation-matching specials by large corporations, so be sure to check for those options when setting up a project. Be sure to check with your school or district before setting up a Donors Choose project, as some schools have specific guidelines around the use of the site.

Back in October of 2015 Billy had two projects funded through Donors Choose; here is an example of what wrote for the project descriptions.

Sample Project Description:

Helping Little Learners with LittleBits – Part 1

My students need a littleBits Arduino Coding and Deluxe Kit to learn about coding with hands-on experiences. This will help them learn valuable 21st-century skills.

Students will have the opportunity to use the littleBits during STEAM Lab and during other open STEAM periods that are currently being worked into the schedule. Students in the Gifted and Talented program will also benefit from these materials as well. Our students are really interested in learning about coding. Due to a tight budget we are limited to what we can order. We want to create an area where students can explore what they are interested in learning. This requested littleBits kit will allow students to build background knowledge with coding. As we learn more about coding we can expand upon this littleBits kit. LittleBits will also encourage Science and Technology classes to utilize the media center, and we can pair projects with littleBits and circuit related research.

Having littleBits would be a step in the right direction of ensuring that my students will get to experience hands on 21st-century learning through STEAM curriculum.

Their love of learning needs to be supported in every way possible. Please help me level the playing field for my students by donating to this project today.

Creating a STEAM/makerspace Lab

My students need supplies such as Arduino Beginner's Kit Bundle, the Cardboard Box Book, copper tape, LED lights and batteries to become makers.

My Project

Help us become the first school in our district to create a makerspace. We are looking to give the opportunity to our students to create, build, and learn. Students will have the opportunity to learn about coding through the use the Arduino Beginner's Kit Bundle and the makers supplies during STEAM Lab and during other open STEAM periods that are currently being worked into the schedule. Students in the Gifted and Talented program will also benefit from these materials. Our students are really interested in learning about coding and making. Due to a tight budget we are limited to what we can order. We want to create an area where students can explore what they are interested in learning. This requested Arduino Beginner's Kit Bundle will allow students to build background knowledge with coding. Students will gain important 21st-century skills with the makers' supplies that will help them become college and career ready.

Having Arduino Beginner's Kit Bundle and makers would be a step in the right direction of ensuring that my students will get to experience hands on 21st-century learning through STEAM curriculum.

Their love of learning needs to be supported in every way possible. Please help me level the playing field for my students by donating to this project today.

Another crowdfunding site is Pledge Cents. This site also has a strong educational side to it, and allows schools and teachers to raise funds for projects, supplies, and events. You may also want to check out Go Fund Me as an option.

There are many STEM and STEAM specific grant opportunities available. www.stemfinity.com/STEM-Education-Grants has a large list of both state specific and national STEM grants. The National Education Association (NEA) also provides STEM grants, with information on their website: www.neafoundation.org/for-districts/stem/. Many corporations provide grants, including Lockheed Martin, Lego, Pearson, and more.

In addition to grants and crowdfunding sites, don't forget to reach out to local businesses and check to see about school foundation grants. Many are willing to donate funds or supplies for needy classrooms. Hardware stores like Lowe's and Home Depot are often happy to work with local schools and classrooms, but don't forget to check in with small businesses as well. It helps to have a specific project or need in mind when approaching these businesses, and having a short write-up of your request on school letterhead is often useful. There are many school districts that have school foundation grants that teachers sometimes are not aware of, or forget to apply to. These are, also, other avenue you can try.

Reflection Questions

- What supplies do you already have on hand for your new STEAM program?
- What will you need? How will you source your supplies?
- Think about local businesses in your area. Which one(s) can you reach out to for funding or supplies?

4

Planning for Instruction

How Do I Plan a STEAM Lesson?

The question many teachers are always wondering is exactly, How do I go about planning for a STEAM lesson? It is not as scary as one might think and can be simple if you follow the steps we include. We have also provided several outlines that can be used when planning a STEAM lesson.

When creating a STEAM lesson, there are several questions that should be asked before we begin designing the lesson or activity. Is this going to be a stand-alone lesson, will you be adding this lesson to another lesson you have already created and planned, or are you going to be planning a large unit that incorporates several smaller activities? If you are planning on incorporating the lesson into a well-established lesson, then hold on, and we will explain that in section C. This section will be geared toward planning that whole class STEAM lesson.

There are several key factors that go into designing a STEAM lesson. Teachers should consider what they want the outcome of the lesson to be. What do they want students to learn or understand over the course of this activity? It's important to consider what materials and supplies you will need for the lesson and where you will get them from. Other key items to consider while planning are the length of time needed to complete the activity, how you plan to assess the activity, and how the activity aligns to state and national standards.

Educators can often feel overwhelmed when trying to develop a STEAM lesson or unit. A major cause of this is the mistaken belief that STEAM lessons must include all of the subjects in the acronym. While it is certainly possible to include all five subjects in one lesson, it is not always possible or practical, particularly for shorter lessons and activities. Instead of trying to incorporate every part of STEAM in every lesson, the key is to develop lessons that blend at least two or three of the components and to vary the way the subjects are combined over the course of several lessons so that students can see how the various subjects can be integrated in a variety of ways.

Planning STEAM Units

The planning for STEAM projects varies depending on the type of project. Sometimes, the projects are smaller, one-off activities designed to highlight a particular concept or support a unit being taught in a core-subject classroom. Other times, a larger STEAM unit is designed that will incorporate several smaller activities followed by one large culminating activity. Later in the chapter we will show you how to plan for those smaller or stand-alone STEAM activities.

The project based school that Meredith teaches at uses a form of backward design called Understanding by Design to plan their units. This method was developed by Jay McTighe and Grant Wiggins, and is explained in depth in their book *Understanding by Design*. The main idea of backward design is to start with the expected outcomes for your students, and plan back from there with the final section of planning being the individual activities that will be completed by the students.

Let's take a look at how the planning of a sample unit works using backward design with incorporating the components of STEAM. Often times, educators get caught up on the concepts of STEAM and do not realize that the lessons they are currently doing have many of the STEAM components incorporated into the lessons. It is just a matter of taking a closer look at the lesson and looking for those components. In this example, students are going to complete a unit on computer programming. There are two main ideas to consider at the beginning of the unit: Understandings (what specifically should students be able to understand after completing the unit?) and Essential Questions (what thought-provoking questions will foster meaning-making, inquiry and transfer?) In the case of the programming unit, these two items looked like this:

Understandings:
- Understand how computers work;

- Understand that a computer program is a sequence of instructions written in a programming language designed to perform a task;
- Understand the roles of computers, programmers and user.

Next we need to ask our Essential Questions.

Essential Questions
- How do computers do what they do?
- Does order matter?
- What do you do when things don't go the way you planned?

Once the Understandings and Essential Questions have been developed, we narrow down what knowledge and skills we want students to acquire as part of this lesson and incorporate key components of STEAM.

Students Will Know ...
- Programming is a sequence of steps (an algorithm). *Here is both our Science and Math Standards. Oftentimes the standards in a STEAM lesson may overlap with one another;*
- How to drag and drop code. *Our technology students are using the computers in order to complete the task;*
- Basic vocabulary words: input, output, the operating system, debug, and algorithm.

Students Will Be Skilled At ...
- Using computational thinking to problem solve using computer programming.

From here, we begin to develop the evaluations both formal and informal that will help us measure student understanding and progress and finally the daily activities that will comprise the unit. See Table 4.1 for a sample activity guide.

This unit provides many opportunities for both formative and summative assessments. The final project, which comprises a significant portion of the grade for the unit, is scored using the rubric in Table 4.2.

Creating a rubric for a STEAM lesson can often be the most difficult part of the lesson. While you can customize a rubric in many ways, the categories to be graded as shown above are a good starting point for most STEAM activities. Whether you use the categories above, or a different style of rubric, one of the keys is consistency across lessons. Whenever possible,

Table 4.1 Sample activity guide for this unit

Day	Activities and Notes
Day 1	Discuss the roles of computers, programmers and users
	◆ Exercise #1: General opening questions about computers
Day 2	How do computers process information?
	◆ Exercise #1: Brainstorm how daily digital devices take and process information
	◆ Exercise #2: Discuss the roles of a user and a computer programmer
Day 3	Design sets of instructions for literal-minded machines
	◆ Exercise #1: Drawing from instructions
Day 4	Design sets of instructions for literal-minded machines
	◆ Exercise #2: Give and follow instructions
Day 5	Design sets of instructions for literal-minded machines
	◆ Exercise #3: Describe how to make a peanut butter and jelly sandwich
Day 6	Get started with Scratch
	◆ Exercise #1: Opening discussion
	◆ Exercise #2: Intro to Scratch: Create something surprising!
Day 7	Get started with Scratch
	◆ Exercise #3: 10 Block challenge
Day 8	Scratch Program #1
	◆ Dancing Cat
Day 9	Scratch Program #2
	◆ Flying Parrot
Day 10	Scratch Program #3
	◆ Shark Chomp game
Day 11	Build an interactive project in Scratch (final project of the unit)
	◆ Unit 1 Final Project: Create a game/animation/story in Scratch
Day 12	Build an interactive project in Scratch (final project of the unit)
	◆ Unit 1 Final Project: Create a game/animation/story in Scratch

(Continued)

Table 4.1 (Continued)

Day	Activities and Notes
Day 13	Build an interactive project in Scratch (final project of the unit)
	◆ Unit 1 Final Project: Create a game/animation/story in Scratch
Day 14	Build an interactive project in Scratch (final project of the unit)
	◆ Unit 1 Final Project: Create a game/animation/story in Scratch
Day 15	Reflection - Journaling / Discussion about programs

it is helpful to use the same "skeleton" for your rubric and simply change the criteria in each of the boxes to fit the individual lessons. By keeping your categories consistent across lessons, students become more familiar with the rubric and what is expected for each lesson. Another benefit of a consistent rubric is that as students become more comfortable with the rubric used in class, they can help develop the rubric with the teacher, giving them increasing ownership of the lesson and what is expected of them.

The addition of the arts to the more traditional STEM curriculum can make it challenging for teachers who may feel they don't have the background to assess artistic skills, or who have concerns about the subjectivity of art. One easy way to solve this is to collaborate with your school's art or music teacher. STEAM is a great way create cross-classroom projects! Teachers can either work together on a single lesson, or create a larger unit that has elements taught in different classes.

Collaboration with teachers who have an expertise in the arts is an ideal solution, but in the real world of teaching, it is not always practical or possible. How, then, can you accurately assess student work in areas you are not strong in? There are two main ways to accomplish this. One method is to determine at the start of the lesson the key skills or outcomes you want to see during the course of the lesson or unit and to grade for their presence or absence. These specific skills or outcomes can be detailed in the Knowledge section of the rubric.

The second method is to focus less on the finished product, and more on the process of getting to the finished product. It is important to keep in mind that rather than assessing the final artistic outcome, you can focus on assessing the essential understandings that are necessary in order to produce the finished product. As an example, in a unit on creating stop-motion

Table 4.2 Teacher rubric – intro to programming.

	Exceeds Expectations	Meets Expectations	Approaches Expectations	Does Not Meet Expectations
Design	* Student included all required items with great attention to detail. Student went beyond the requirements to include more information	* Student included all required items with attention to detail beyond the basics	* Student included all required items, but showed minimal effort and little detail	* Student did not complete one or more of the required items for their project
Knowledge	* Project shows advanced understanding of blocks and procedures	* Project shows understanding of blocks and how they work together to meet a goal	* Project shows some understanding of blocks and how they work together	* Project shows little understanding of blocks and how they work together
Application	* Uses additional programming techniques * Is particularly well organized, logical, and debugged	* Is organized, logical, and debugged	* Has some organization and logic * May have a couple bugs	* Lacks organization and logic * Has several bugs
Process	* Used project time constructively, finished early or added additional elements * Found ways to collaborate beyond class structure	* Used project time constructively, met deadlines * Collaborated appropriately	* Used project time well sometimes and met some deadlines * Collaborated at times	* Did not use project time well and did not meet deadlines * Did not collaborate
Presentation	* Well-rehearsed with smooth delivery that holds audience attention * Content is well organized and groups related material	* Rehearsed with fairly smooth delivery that holds audience attention most of the time * Uses some form of organization, but the overall organization of topics appears flawed	* Delivery not smooth, but able to maintain interest of the audience most of the time * Content is logically organized for the most part	* Delivery not smooth and audience attention often lost * There was no clear or logical organizational structure, just lots of facts

TOTAL POINTS

animation videos, part of the Design assessment on the rubric focused on how much time and detail were put into the sets and characters used in the film. The assessment had little to do with how artistic the designs were, or the final quality of them, but rather emphasized student understanding that having a good set and character design were important to the overall quality of the film. Art is very subjective, and student skills will vary widely. Emphasizing the importance of the underlying understandings necessary for the art rather than the final design or product is a way for teachers who may not have a strong art background to fairly assess student art and design work.

One major benefit of grading by rubric, especially one like the sample above, is that it allows students who may struggle with one aspect of a project a way to show strength in other areas. A student who has trouble with the Application section of the rubric may make up points with a strong presentation. By breaking down the grading into specifically delineated categories on the rubric, students are also aware of what exactly they need to do to earn a specific grade, and it is easy for the teacher to explain the specifics of why they received the grade they did.

Managing My Time with a Tight Schedule

Time is often the question that is brought up by teachers, as teachers need to jam pack so many different topics into a short period of time. When planning and implementing STEAM into the classroom, a teacher wants to be able to get the lesson into an already tight schedule. One of the biggest components of teaching STEAM is group work and having students be able to work collaboratively with each other.

- The Facilitator provides leadership and direction for the group, leads discussions, suggests solutions to team problems, helps members clarify points, protects members from attack, makes sure that every voice is heard, focuses work on the learning task, says, "Let's hear from____next," says, "That is interesting, but let's get back to our task."[1]
- The Recorder keeps a public record of the team's ideas and progress. They will check to be sure that ideas are clear and accurate. The recorder possibly uses charts, multiple colors, and other techniques to highlight and summarize the ideas of the team. The recorder will say, "I think I heard you say____; is that right?" says, "How would you like me to write this?" The recorder will also synthesize the group's final idea.

- The Summarizer restates the group's conclusions and responses, prepares a summary of the group's efforts, checks for clarity of understanding, says, "Does this accurately reflect what we have done today?" says, "Have I left out anything important here?" Will synthesize the group's ideas.
- Timer – Keeps a group of the amount of time left.
- Reflector – Will have group reflect upon work by asking the group one of the questions from the list of "Reflection Questions."
- The Equipment Manager – Will make sure the group has the correct materials to use for the idea and the correct challenge.

Billy has used these rules in his classroom and he has found that they work well with his students. Keep in mind that there are many different ways in which to manage your time. The biggest advice we can give is to make sure your lesson is well planned out and that you allow for the unexpected, as it always occurs during a STEAM lesson. It might be a student discovering something new or a different way in which to complete a project or a task. This is all GOOD – as STEAM educators, you want your students to explore and create and grow. Time is always against us in the education world, but a good, planned out lesson and a little flexibility can become an amazing learning experience for students.

Student-Centered Lesson

Student-centered lessons are becoming the new norm in education. How do we get students to develop their own lessons and explore ways in which they want to learn? Students can be the ones to drive their learning; we just need to give them the tools to create their own learning experiences. Empower your students to create lessons in which they are guiding their exploration. Managing a class of 24 or more students can always be challenging. How do you manage a class during a STEAM lesson to make sure, as Meredith says, a student is not on fire? We will explore different ways in which to make this a fun learning experience and non-stressful experience for the educator. In the next chapter, we'll walk through facilitating a sample STEAM lesson, and include troubleshooting tips for common problems. We will discuss student roles and responsibilities, as well as how to work your students up to becoming self-directed learners.

How will you manage your STEAM lesson? Do you have a creative way to get students to develop their own lesson? Please use the #GSwSTEAM to share your ideas or borrow an idea from another educator.

Reflection Questions

- What lesson are you going to plan for STEAM?
- What are the different components you need to include?

Note

1. www.dailyteachingtools.com/cooperative-learning-tasks.html www.readwritethink.org/files/resources/lesson_images/lesson277/cooperative.pdf

5

Incorporating the Core Subjects

Incorporating Language Arts (Writing and Reading) into STEAM

STEAM can be incorporated into lesson plans more easily than most educators might think. It takes a little tweaking, a little bit of Internet searching, and a little bit of planning, but it can create an experience of learning that students will remember. As we go through this section of the chapter, we will discuss ways in which to incorporate STEAM into a lesson plan. The focus in this section will be how we can incorporate Language Arts into STEAM and have the A mean language Arts.

STEAM can be done without spending hours redoing a current lesson. The planning template that we have provided in this section is just one way in which you can start on your STEAM adventures.

The A in STEAM does not just have to stand just for Art but can stand for Language Arts. Literacy can dovetail nicely into almost any STEAM activity. One of the easiest (although not only) ways to incorporate this is with a writing component. Students can learn about technical and scientific writing while documenting the process of an activity or writing up a report at the end. Storytelling can also factor into many STEAM lessons. Students can create stop-motion animation stories using computers, cell phones, or digital cameras. They can also create plays or skits to share what they have learned or created. Students can use outlining skills to plan projects. The list is never-ending. There are also hundreds of books that can be incorporated into a STEAM curriculum. From recreating fairy tales as mentioned earlier in this book, to using books like *Rosie Revere, Engineer* by Andrea Beaty, the possibilities of combining literature and STEAM are endless.

Let's return to a classic story such as "The Three Little Pigs". First, let's break down the components of STEAM, since we do not always have to use all of the components to be teaching our students STEAM. Let's take a look at what components were used. With "The Three Little Pigs", you first can read the story to the students and discuss the differences about fairy tales, so right off the back we are using the A in STEAM, and we are discussing the arts as part of the Language Arts as we are reading the story to our students. They are developing listening skills that are an important part of Language Arts, and as the teacher, depending on the grade level you are teaching, you can incorporate different reading and writing skills.

Next, we are going to have our students become engineers and designers as our students will be designing houses for the three little pigs. The engineering can fall under both the S and the E as part of the Next Generation Science standards is to have students engineer a design. Students will be using their math skills to figure out how big of a house they can create with the supplies they have.

The materials that you need for the project are 50 straws, 50 popsicles sticks, and 50 index cards and one yard of masking tape they are then asked to create a house that will withstand the Big Bad Wolf (the classroom fan). Time is always an issue in the classroom as we never have enough of the time, the theory is time can be flexible these projects do not have to be done in one shot and done deal. You can have these projects go on for a few days or few weeks. Whatever best fits your schedule: we are just giving you ideas which you can incorporate into your teaching. If you do not have as much time, give students five minutes to design, five minutes to collaborate on the design and then 20 minutes to create their design (Table 5.1).

Table 5.1 Breakdown of STEAM components for "The Three Little Pigs"

S	Next Generation Science Standards – Engineering and Designing
T	Technology can be having students write a post reflection on a computer or taking videos of their projects
E	Engineer is designing and developing houses
A	Language Arts the story being read to the students and reading skills being brought in.
M	How big of a house do I need to make, how much of my materials do I need to use?

There are a lot of easy ways to include language arts in STEAM. A great way to incorporate technology into literature is to have students use or create Google lit trips. These are interactive maps that include points of interest from famous stories and novels. For example, one well-known Google lit trip is based on the book *Make Way for Ducklings* by Robert McCloskey. On the map, students can follow the trail of the duck family as they travel through historic Boston, and also learn about historic figures and places in the town. Students and teachers can download lit trips from the Google lit trips website, or they can create their own for whatever book or story they are working on.

Book trailers are another great way to incorporate language arts into steam. In book trailers students can use simple tech tools such as slides or video to create a trailer for a book that they have read. Just like movies have trailers to entice people to come see them, your students can create book trailers about books in your library or books that you've read as a class in order to encourage others to read them. A simple video tool such as wevideo.com can be used to create a book trailer with very little prior experience. You can also use simple slideshow tools such as Google Slides, Keynote, or PowerPoint to create these book trailers.

Novel Engineering is another program designed to help teachers combine engineering and math skills along with literacy. "Students use existing classroom literature – stories, novels, and expository texts – as the basis for engineering design challenges that help them identify problems, design realistic solutions, and engage in the Engineering Design Process while reinforcing their literacy skills."[1]

The students in Meredith's school in Philadelphia created a great STEAM project for their Humanities class. They had been reading several graphic novels on the theme of bravery, and as their final project were incorporating what they learned about bravery with places and people in their neighborhood of West Philadelphia. As part of this project students researched various historical places and people in Philadelphia and put together a write-up about them and why they fit the theme of "bravery". Students then created short podcast recordings about their historic place or person. These podcasts were then linked to an interactive map of the city. At the end of the project, families and community members were invited to join the students for a walking tour of the city where they could use this interactive map and listen to the podcasts as they reached each important spot on the map.

If you're not ready to dive into such large-scale projects, remember that literacy can be part of any subject. Students can hone their writing skills by writing up their project plans, process, and results. They can also create presentations to tell others about what they have accomplished. Students can also increase their skills in speaking and listening as they present to others in the class.

Incorporating Technology

As we mentioned previously, technology is a word that is often synonymous with computers. It is important to keep in mind, however, that they are only one aspect of technology. Technology is an extremely broad category that includes so much more than just computers. If you have ready access to computers, they are definitely a great tool to help with STEAM lessons. Don't be discouraged, however, if you do not have ready access for your students. Let's take a look at how we can incorporate various types of technology to support the Arts aspect of STEAM.

Mobile phones are a great technology tool that are often underused in the classroom. While districts vary in their policies and approaches to using student phones in schools, if you have the opportunity to allow your students to use these as part of the lesson, do so. At the very least, phones can be used to access the web for research and information, but they are capable of so much more. Leaving aside the thousands of apps available for education, the phone's camera capabilities make it a fantastic tool for documenting projects and experiments. Students can take photographs of the steps they took in an activity and create a how-to guide for future classes. They can use pictures of their projects in their presentations at the end of a project. They can also create stop-motion or action videos to document their progress and achievements. Phones can also be used for note-taking, audio recording and editing, and much more.

In that vein, if cell phone use is not permitted, inexpensive digital cameras can be used for much of the same, and are an invaluable tool in the classroom. There are so many creative and useful ways for students to use images and videos as part of their projects, so give them a camera and set them loose.

Digital audio recorders can also be a useful piece of technology in the STEAM classroom. They can be used for a variety of tasks, from taking audio notes to recording interviews with fellow students and outside experts. They can also be used to record voiceovers for videos and slideshows.

It is also important to consider technology in the form of software. Again, while there are tons of great apps and programs designed specifically for STEAM, don't overlook the obvious. Student or class blogs are a great way for your kids to document their learning and to share it with others. Similarly, a class or individual student website is another way to document and share with a wider audience. A simple tool like Kidblog, Google Sites, or Wordpress also allows for lessons that incorporate digital citizenship, layout, publishing, and more.

There are also tons of tech tools and devices available, from digital whiteboards to MakeyMakey circuit boards to document cameras, and much much more. The most important thing to remember is that while these gadgets and tools are wonderful, the definition of technology is so much broader. According, in part, to Merriam-Webster, the definition of "technology" includes:

- the practical application of knowledge especially in a particular area;
- a manner of accomplishing a task especially using technical processes, methods, or knowledge. [2]

Don't get so hung up on a particular device that you forget the overarching aspects of technology.

Incorporating the Arts

The main thing that separates STEM from STEAM is the incorporation of the arts. One of the exciting things about incorporating the arts is the broad variety of ways you can include them. STEAM lessons can include visual arts, performing arts, language arts, and more. The arts can be a large part of a lesson, or a small part. This flexibility makes it easy to include art of some kind into almost any lesson.

One of the easiest ways to begin including the arts into STEAM lessons and activities is to make it part of a final project or presentation. In the earlier section on Design Thinking, art was included in several ways as part of the sample lesson. Drawing and design skills were used in the middle of the Extraordinaires project as students learned about technical drawing and created their formal design drawings. Modeling and design skills were used for the final portion of the Extraordinaires activity as students designed and built their prototype models.

Another example of incorporating art into STEAM goes along with a lesson on catapults. Students learn about math, physics, and engineering while designing and testing catapults, and then use the catapults they build to launch paint-dipped pom-poms at paper or canvas to create catapult art. Keep in mind that the design of the catapults themselves is also a form of art!

Robotics and art also go together extremely well. Students can use programs such as Scratch or Tynker to explore the intersections of math and art. From creating an app to design freehand art, to creating one that uses geometric shapes to create collages and murals, programming and art go hand in hand. Students can also create their own physical art – Sphero robots dipped in washable paint can be programmed to create large-scale murals and designs. A plastic cup, some rubber bands, some markers, and a small vibration motor can be combined to create simple draw-bots that combine electronics, engineering, and art and are simple enough for even young students to create and use.

Want to incorporate performing arts? Why not have your students learn about musical instruments and design their own using everyday materials? From popsicle stick harmonicas to cardboard tube kazoos to tin can banjos to thumb pianos, there are so many great ways to design playable instruments while exploring science and math topics such as sound waves, engineering, vibrations, and more. Wrap up the lesson with a performance by your new classroom orchestra!

Incorporating Engineering

In the Next Generation Science Standards, engineering has become a focal part with the Engineering Design Process. Students need to ask questions and define a problem. They may ask themselves: what is the problem we need to solve? and what materials do we have to use? Students might have to plan out and carry out an investigation. They might ask themselves: how can we create a solution? or how do we start to build a design? In the engineering process, students need to construct explanations and design a solution to a problem. Students might ponder the design, and might ask themselves why did it work or why did it not work? Is there a way to redesign and improve what we have? These steps are important to the engineering design process. A simple project that Billy has used with his students to get them to start thinking like an engineer is a car challenge that he tweaked from http://pbskids.org/designsquad/build/4-wheel-balloon-car.

How do we get students to act like scientists and get "a square peg to fit into a round hole" like the challenge the astronauts faced on the Apollo 13 mission? Develop a challenge for students where they are given certain materials and only allowed to use those materials they have to create an item that is functional. Keep in mind that you can use a bunch of materials with your students and give them different challenges. The idea is to get the students to think critically.

The objective that was given to the students was as follows: create a new car that needs to be powered without polluting the environment. The students were shown the materials that they were allowed to use butthey were not able to start building right away because a good engineer needs to develop a plan before they can start to build. Keep in mind that this is just one idea of the materials that students can use; most of these materials can be found around a house or a school or can be purchased at the dollar store. The materials they were given were: toilet-paper tube, paper towel tube, flexible straw, bottle caps, play dough, gloves and a plastic bag, rubber bands, straws, paperclips. Students were told that they would NOT get extra materials but they did not need to use all of the materials they had to develop a car that would not pollute the environment but would work. Students were given worksheets to help develop their ideas. An alternative to using worksheets and integrating computers would be to use Google Drawing for G Suite Schools or any school with access to Google Drawings, Paint on a PC device, Sketch Pad on a Surface Tablet or Artboard for an Apple Device.

Students were also given questions to think about during their planning phase. These questions were: "How can you get the car to move?" and "How do you get the car to stay together using the materials you have?" In the **Planning Phase**, students would meet and come up with a design for their car. They will need either scrap paper or writing space below the directions to complete this task. The directions were:

> Meet as a team and discuss how you can create a car out of the materials you. Then develop and agree on a design for your car.

In the **Creation Phase**, students would build their cars using the materials provided. During the **Testing Phase**, students would collect the data at the testing phase using a simple chart. After students have completed the testing phase and have several results, they can choose to either redesign their car or they can move onto the next phase which is the **Evaluation Phase**. In this phase, students evaluate their teams' results. Here are the sample questions that Billy has used in the past:

1. Did you succeed in creating a car that can travel on the floor? If so, how far did it travel? If not, why did it fail?
2. Did you decide to revise your original design? Why?

3. If you could have had access to materials that were different from those provided, what would your team have requested? Why?
4. Do you think that engineers have to adapt their original plans during the construction of systems or products? Why might they?

This is just one example of a simple to-do project in which you can incorporate engineering into STEAM. Billy and Meredith love to use PBS Design Squad to gain ideas for incorporating Engineering. Check out the website for other ideas here http://pbskids.org/designsquad/.

Incorporating Social Studies

There are many great ways to include social studies as part of STEAM. Ancient cultures are a great starting point for STEAM lessons. Learning about Ancient Rome? Have students build an aqueduct. Recreate a Roman road. Buff up on architecture skills by designing ancient or modern buildings using different types of Roman columns. Is Ancient Egypt your topic? Learn about the mummification process by mummifying apple slices! Who can design the tallest pyramid using toothpicks and mini marshmallows or clay?

Learning about maps? 3D topographic maps help students grasp the underlying concepts of these types of maps. They are VERY easy to make. All you need are some foam sheets in different colors, scissors, glue, sharpies, and printouts of topographic maps from Google Images.

Students started by choosing a map and cutting it out along the outer line. They then put the cutout on the foam, traced it, and cut it out. Then, they trimmed their paper map along the next line in, and repeated the process. Each subsequent layer of the map was glued down, with each layer a different color. When they finished, they had beautiful 3D topographic maps to display in the classroom (Figure 5.1).

Incorporating Math

It is great fun incorporating math into STEAM. Not only can math be found in all sorts of projects and activities, it is also a lot more engaging for students than worksheets and drills. One fun math activity for students is making parabolic curves. This is a pretty neat visual lesson, because we are going to make a "curved" line using only straight lines. We get our curves by connecting points that are equally spaced along lines meeting in a right angle. The more points, the more curved your parabola will appear (Figure 5.2).

Figure 5.1 3D topographic map

Figure 5.2 Finished parabolic curve

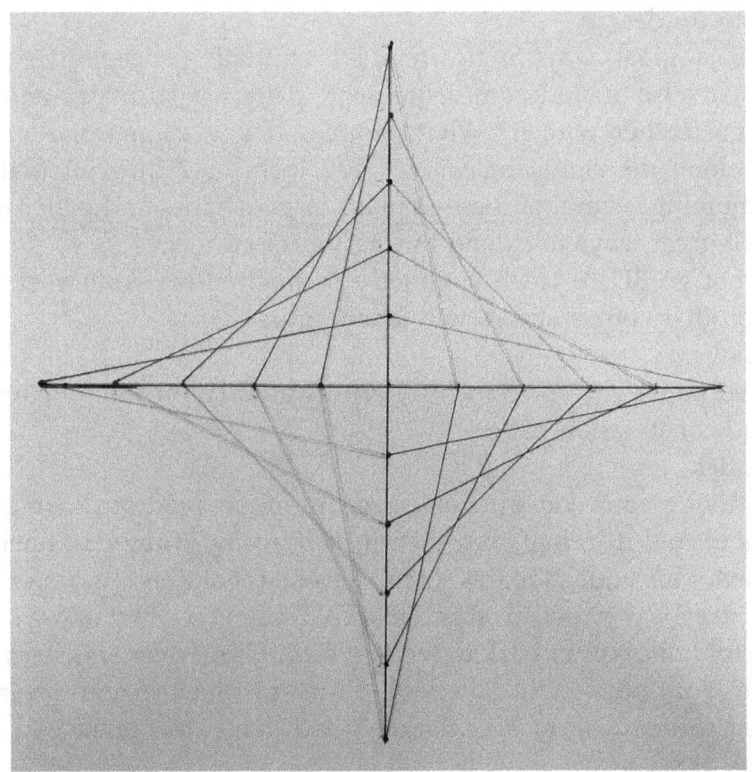

1. To begin, find the center of your 12 × 12 paper. I find it easiest to fold it in half twice, then open it up. Where the folds meet is the center. Use your pencil to mark the center with a dot.
2. Next, place your ruler across the center of the paper with the dot at the 5-inch mark. Draw a line that is 10 inches long, with the dot in the center of it.
3. Repeat this in the other direction to make a plus sign.
4. Now, start at the center dot, and mark one inch intervals along one leg until you have five marks.
5. Repeat for each leg. Then, starting at the dot, lightly number the marks 1–5, with the one always being the closest to the center dot and the five always being at the farthest point of the leg.
6. It's time to start making our parabolic curve! You are going to use the ruler to connect the marks that add up to 6 for each of the quadrants. (5 + 1, 4 + 2, etc.)
7. Notice that although we used only straight lines, it looks like a curve! Now it's time to finish it up. Break out the gel pens or markers (fine point is best) and go over your penciled-in lines to create your work of art. You can also try shading in some of the boxes if you want.
8. Last, you can go back and erase your pencil marks to leave just your colorful design.

This is a great way to tie in a lot of math concepts. Beyond just parabolas, it also includes measurement, patterns, addition, and angles. Want to go further with it? What happens if you change the size of the intervals along the right angles? Try 1/2 inch, or 2 inch intervals. What about combining several of these to make larger shapes and patterns? There are a lot of great ways to extend this easy project.

Why not go 3D to teach symmetry in math? This is another fun and easy lesson that your students will love (Figure 5.3).

Materials:

Colored paper cut into 3 inch squares (I used colored copy paper)

12 × 12 construction paper

Glue stick

First, divide your construction paper into four quadrants. An easy way to do it is to fold it in half, and then in half again. When you open it, you should have four equal squares. Now, let's start folding our paper "darts". We'll use the 3 × 3 paper for this. First, fold the paper in half.

Next, fold one corner back to the first fold. Flip it over and repeat on the other side. Your paper will now look a little bit like a paper airplane. The two folded corners will make a flat diamond shape, this is the end you will glue to the paper.

Figure 5.3 3D symmetry example

While you can fold and glue the darts one at a time, I find it easier to make a pile of darts first, then start gluing. Since we are working on symmetry, you'll want at least four darts of each color.

OK, time to assemble! Students start in the center of the paper and begin gluing down the darts with the glue stick. Remember that what you create in one quadrant must be repeated exactly in the other three to keep the symmetry.

There are many ways to combine your darts to make symmetrical shapes and patterns. When you are finished, compare how many different patterns your class created.

Another great math activity that is very hands-on is using Lego blocks to teach area and perimeter. Lego blocks can be used for a lot of math concepts; another favorite is using them to learn fractions! There are a lot of great ways to incorporate math in STEAM. Get creative!

Language-Art Resources

One of Billy's go-to places for STEAM fairy tale lessons is Tara Lazar's (@taralazar) Pinterest page, for other ways to incorporate fairy tales into your STEAM lessons. (www.pinterest.com/taralazar/fairy-tales-for-stem-steam/ (also make sure to check out Cybraryman's website on Fairy Tales http://cybraryman.com/fairytales.html).

Reflection Questions

- How are you going to incorporate the arts?
- What type of technology will you include in your lesson?

Notes

1. "Novel Engineering – Home |." www.novelengineering.org. Accessed 26 Dec. 2017.
2. "Technology | Definition of Technology by Merriam-Webster." www.merriam-webster.com/dictionary/technology. Accessed 26 Jun. 2017.

6

Getting Aligned
Standards and Assessments

Getting aligned to the standards is an important aspect to plan for as educators. Most schools and districts require lessons to be standards-aligned, whether with the Next Generation Science Standards (NGSS), the Common Core State Standards (CCSS), ISTE's Standards for Students, or your local state standards. One of the great aspects of STEAM education is that you can pull in standards for a variety of subjects for most lessons and activities. How and when you align standards with your lessons may vary from person to person, and activity to activity. Sometimes, you may have an awesome lesson that fits perfectly with what you are trying to teach your students, and you search out the standards that will fit with that particular activity. Other times, you may be trying to address a specific standard or set of standards and designing your lesson around them. Whichever way you go about aligning your lessons, having a STEAM lesson will allow you the opportunity to address cross-disciplinary standards.

Two of the top questions asked by those considering starting a makerspace or STEM lab are, Can I align activities to the standards? and How do I assess student work? There are many views on whether and how to align with standards and assess students. Some choose to avoid these two aspects, but most schools and districts require some level of alignment and assessment. This section will walk you through different types of assessments that can be done from makers projects along with how to align to the

Common Core standards and the Next Generation Science Standards (www.nextgenscience.org/).

Billy and Meredith believe that the project itself should not be assessed, but the students who are doing the work should be assessed. One question that is asked is, Can't I just grade if the student completes the task? The problem with that is what if the student fails the task but can work together with other students; shouldn't they be graded on that? We have looked at many different rubrics and have found one that we like the best, which is a generic rubric that can be used for many different projects. See the STEAM Activity Rubric for an example of ways in which you can assess your students without having to assess their projects.

The car challenge as we discussed in Chapter 5 can easily be aligned with the *Next Generation Science Standard 3.5-ETS1-1-*: "Define a simple design problem reflecting a need or want that includes specified criteria for success and constraints on materials, time, or cost." Many STEAM and maker projects are easily aligned with many of the Next Generation Science Standards and along with many of the Common Core Standards that several states have adopted. If your state is not using one of these standards, take a quick look at your standards and see where you can fit a project into. It might seem at hard first, but from our experience, it just takes a little bit of time and some creativity.

Don't let the word "science" limit your use of these standards. Many of the skills addressed in these standards are applicable across multiple subjects. For example, looking at the Middle School standards for *MS-PS2 Motion and Stability: Forces and Interactions*, the accompanying Science and Engineering practices include "Asking Questions and Defining Problems, Planning and Carrying Out Investigations, Constructing Explanations and Designing Solutions, and Engaging in Argument from Evidence." These are all strong science concepts, but can also be applied in a much broader range of core subjects from math, to language arts, to social studies, and more.

Many writing standards can also be aligned with a STEAM unit or activity. Meredith feels it is important to include some type of writing assignment with most activities. These can be simple or more complex. Students need to not only be able to complete a STEAM activity, but also be able to communicate what they have done and learned. This is also a good way to teach students about technical and scientific writing; skills too often neglected in a traditional language-arts classroom. There are a variety of ways to accomplish this depending on the project and what the teacher wants the students to focus on. In some cases, Meredith has students keep a design journal that they write daily during a larger unit to track their progress, failures, and successes. In other cases, students may be asked to write a reflection on the activity and answer specific questions about their learning. Students can also create presentations to share what they have learned, or even incorporate creative writing, such as creating a skit or crafting a narrative around a particular lesson or activity.

Another set of standards that tie in very well with STEAM lessons are ISTE's Standards For Students. While many teachers consider ISTE to be purely technology-related, a look at the 2016 standards show a variety of cross-curricular skills are included in these new standards. For the purposes of STEAM lessons, one of the sections that is most relevant is

ISTE Standard 4. Innovative Designer

Students use a variety of technologies within a design process to identify and solve problems by creating new, useful or imaginative solutions. Students:

a. know and use a deliberate design process for generating ideas, testing theories, creating innovative artifacts or solving authentic problems.
b. select and use digital tools to plan and manage a design process that considers design constraints and calculated risks.
c. develop, test and refine prototypes as part of a cyclical design process.
d. exhibit a tolerance for ambiguity, perseverance and the capacity to work with open-ended problems.

The other ISTE standards also lend themselves well to certain STEAM projects, but Innovative Designer is the one that fits best across most types of projects. Most projects will be able to incorporate one or more parts of this standard.

Assessment

We have taken you through the important part of planning or incorporating a lesson to become a STEAM lesson and we have discussed the importance of aligning to your state standards. Now let's discuss why the Assessment piece is equally important and why we have included it in this chapter. As we have seen, students are creating their own design and developing their ideas, so the big question becomes: how do I assess my students' work? Well this topic can be debated over and over again. The argument we make is: why are trying to assess student work? How can you assess creativity? It is difficult. We believe in assessing the way in which students have worked with one another on the project, or the steps a student has taken in order to complete the project. What if a student has an amazing design but it fails? Should we fail the student? Let's remember that the Wright brothers failed a number of times before they had a working plane. Did Thomas Edison create a light bulb on his first attempt? NO. So, why are we going to fail a student who tried and developed their own ideas on a project. We have included in Table 6.1 ... a sample assessment of what we believe is a good way to assess students' work on STEAM projects. There are many different ways in which you can assess students but we believe that this rubric is one of the most fair methods.

In almost every classroom, the work of assessment falls on the shoulders of the teacher. While this is usually valid and necessary, consider having students take on some of the assessment tasks as well. There are several ways to incorporate this in a STEAM classroom. One method is to have the student and the teacher both score the project using the same rubric. Once this has been completed, the student and teacher sit down together and compare rubrics and confer over it. If there is a discrepancy between teacher and student scores on the rubric, this opens the door for discussion and gives the student a chance to defend their choices and perhaps provide more evidence towards a higher grade; it is also a chance for the teacher to discuss with the student those areas where they may have struggled or could improve for the next project. This type of shared rubric is a great way to encourage self-reflection at the end of a project. A second method is to have a student rubric for students to score each other on. In this case, the student rubric often focuses on how well their teammates functioned on aspects of collaboration. These can be done anonymously if needed, and are a great way to encourage students to develop their collaboration and teamwork skills (Tables 6.1 and 6.2).

Reflection Question

- What are the ways in which you can incorporate your state standards into STEAM?

Table 6.1 STEM activity rubric

Activity/Challenge:
Student Name: _____
Grade: /20

Category	4	3	2	1
Proactive Problem-solving	Consistently develops and suggest solutions to team members.	Suggests refinements to solutions presented by team members.	Listens to suggestions from team members but does not make any of their own.	Makes no effort to solve problems. Relies on team members to do the work.
Contributions	Provides many contributions to the team. A strong leader.	Provides some contributions to the team when problem-solving and discussing.	Provides few contributions to team problem-solving and discussion.	Provides little to no contributions to the team or refuses to do any of the work.
Attitude	Always has a positive attitude. Actively encourages other team members to stay positive. Never critical of the project to others.	Usually has a positive attitude towards the team and/or work. Rarely critical of the project to others.	Occasionally has a negative attitude towards the team and/or work. Sometimes positive about the project.	Has a negative attitude towards the team and/or work. Is usually critical of the project or the team members.
Focus on the Task	Always completes required work. Assists others in completing their work.	Usually completes required work. Team members can count on them to get their part of the project done.	Sometimes completed the required work. Team members often need to remind the student to stay on-task.	Does not complete required work. Does not participate or interact with other team members.
Working with Others	Almost always works well with other team members. Never critical. Provides strong contributions to the group and supports other team members.	Usually works well with other team members. Rarely critical. Provides regular contributions to the group.	Sometimes works well with team members but often critical. Some contributions to the group.	Rarely/never works well with team members. Few/no contributions to the group.

Comments:

Table 6.2 Sample student rubric

Activity / Challenge: _____
Student Name: _____
Team Members: _____

Objectives	Great! We rocked this!	We did okay – would change things next time	Could have done better
Teamwork			
We used our time wisely	2	1	0
We solved problems in a fair way	2	1	0
We all participated and did our best	2	1	0
Preparation			
Our project was well planned out	2	1	0
We paid great attention to detail	2	1	0
We completed all of the steps in the project	2	1	0
We worked on all parts of the project together	2	1	0
Final Product			
Our project was a success. (Or, if it did not succeed, we were able to explain why and/or fix the problem)	2	1	0
We were able to clearly explain our work and results to others.	2	1	0
We were able to defend decisions we made during the course of the project	2	1	0

Total: _____ out of 20 points

7

It Takes a Village
Getting the Community Involved

Creating a space that is amazing, welcoming, creative, and allows students to learn can take a lot of hard work and dedication as a teacher. However, you do not have to do it all; you should look for support from all stakeholders who are involved. As we discussed in chapter 3, there are a few ways to get donations to stockpile your space, one aspect that is important to look at is getting support from your community and families.

Administration

The key to having a strong STEAM program of any size or shape is administrative buy-in and support. Without the backing of your school or district administration, it can be difficult to launch and maintain a quality program. Before approaching your administration about getting started with STEAM, do some research and planning. Look at what other schools in your area are doing. Have any of them launched a STEAM program, and, if so, can you ask them for support and guidance? Are you going to be the first school in your area to try something like this? How can adding a STEAM program make your school a pioneer?

It also helps to have a clear plan when you approach administration. Consider what we have talked about in previous chapters. Where will the program live? Who will be responsible for planning the lessons? What materials will be needed? Where and how will you store them? How will you handle assessment? Having answers to these questions before you sit down with your administration can make it a lot easier to convince them to try this new approach.

> Fred Ende works as the Assistant Director of Curriculum and Instructional Services for the Putnam Northern Westchester BOCES in Westchester County, New York. Fred has helped develop the maker movement in his region.
>
> Making a Difference: Professional Growth for Makerspace Development
>
> If your region is anything like mine, then there is a tremendous want and need for support related to makerspaces. The Maker movement, as we know, is one that centers on putting the design of learning, and all that comes along with it, ultimately in the hands of the learners themselves. Whether the Making takes the form of putting a pre-existing device together (or taking it apart), solving a problem through the building of a device, or designing a model for something that doesn't yet exist, but could, Making is as much about the process of learning behind the scenes as it is about the product being formed.
>
> In truth, Making is so much more than re-imagining the "Tech" or "Shop" classes of our past. We've learned over the last few years that to appropriately support schools and districts in their journey to make meaning through Making, we need to keep in mind a few important ideas (fun fact: all three of these ideas relate really well to strong professional learning practices in general!).
>
> Expand the view of who can lead Maker initiatives. Early on, as the "Do It Yourself" movement began to come into the spotlight, there was much talk about who was going to take the work on, and what it might look like. Initially, there were wonderings about whether technology education teachers would be "responsible" and whether there was a need for anyone else to focus on Making (maybe the science educators could get involved as well). As we've seen in our region, the vision of a Maker, and who can be tapped to lead students down that path, has grown. Many of our districts now see the library and the library media specialist as a foundation to Making programs in their schools. Library media specialists have often celebrated the chance to further display their talents and include themselves more deeply in the process of learning in schools. Whether tied to the design of a library space, or helping identify and evaluate resources to help with the design process, the vision of a Maker and those with makerspace expertise has broadened tremendously. In fact, our Library Systems Coordinator has taken on the task of designing and supplying some of our Maker support directly through his

library networks. No longer simply in the wheelhouse of technology or science educators, making the most of Making means thinking more broadly about who can lead the work.

Build capacity to sustain capacity. Supporting Maker initiatives in our region is not just about providing details on strategies and skills to help in designing and facilitating a makerspace. One learning we have taken from providing support to districts is that sustaining capacity regarding Maker initiatives is just as important as building it. Our region has put its support behind a collegial circle group made up of makerspace leaders. The members of the group range from teachers, to administrators, to librarians. In fact, our facilitator of the group is a library media specialist from one of our local districts. This collegial circle group is one of the first professional learning offerings we provide to fill each year, and it is consistently one that spurs excellent conversation and important questions for consideration now and into the future. We have also gained further evidence to support the fact that true professional growth does not exist without follow-up learning. Along with this collegial circle, we have worked hard to provide follow-up learning opportunities for those who have already built their initial capacity. Whether it be through a wearable-electronics workshop or a Maker experience tied exclusively to early elementary learners, sustaining is key to long-term growth.

Seeing is believing. As we began to provide assistance around Maker work, we noticed something was missing. Our learning opportunities tended to be led in our regional workshop center, and were often facilitated by consultants; trained, knowledgeable, and well-skilled certainly, yet consultants nonetheless. Over time, we have worked to include visitations of makerspaces into our collegial circle (our lead facilitator sets these up with her members), and we've shifted some of our workshops to be led entirely by teachers immersed in the Making process in their schools. This requires some of the control to be relinquished to someone else, and we have seen our share of challenges as we have made this shift. Yet, from a learning perspective, nothing can beat seeing an idea or strategy in action, from those who are actively practicing, in order to help us shift the way we do things and take action to grow.

makerspaces have tremendous implications to make a difference in the lives of learners (both young and adult). As we consider ways to support the growth of those initiatives, we need to remember that anyone can be a leader in Making. And if we're willing to help people continue their growth and provide opportunities for those we serve to learn from models of good practice, we can support Making (and everything else, really) in ways that lead it to really make meaning for everyone.

As we can see from Fred's example, being able to support at a regional level is important if your region is set up in this way. Not all education systems are set up like this; some education systems only have the elementary and middle-school level and some have elementary, middle school and high-school levels. In those districts you need to look for support from Administration for new initiatives. Take a look at a Chester School District in New Jersey where Brad Currie, the 2017 NASSP National Assistant Principal of The Year, has supported the creation and evolution of two middle school STEM programs over the past decade. Brad has truly been a supportive administrator to his teachers and have brought in many different programs to his Middle School. Let's find out from Brad about those programs.

Supporting STEM in the Middle

The Innovation and Design classes offered to all students are engaging and relevant. Both programs have seen this pre-engineering offering develop from infancy many years ago to one of the most sought after 21st-century learning curricula in the field of science education. Each day, students are exposed to technology-driven and collaborative projects that require higher-level thinking in order to solve challenging tasks.

The sixth grade curriculum incorporates real-world issues with science and technology-based solutions. For example, sixth graders explore the issue of energy use, and have learned that buildings account for half of the energy used in the US. Sixth graders use programs like Tinkercad or SketchUp to design a 3D solar house or object drawn to scale. These programs often allow architects and their clients to visualize green features such as solar panels, sustainable landscaping, and building materials that will serve to produce a more sustainable world. Students also research solar radiation, as well as photovoltaic cells and how they convert the sun's rays into electrical energy. With SketchUp, Google Earth, 3D Printers, and design software, students can create contemporary eco-friendly homes or objects and become even more inspired and educated about reducing their own ecological footprint.

The seventh grade curriculum helps students further their understanding of STEM by applying their sixth grade learning experiences to more challenging issues. Scientists have been trying to understand the effects of earthquakes on structures for years. As student engineers, seventh graders design and build a model structure out of balsa wood that will withstand the stress of a simulated earthquake. The goal is to create a model of a 20-story, 200-foot high building that can withstand an earthquake. Students test their towers using a Programmable Earthquake Tremor Table, then analyze the effects of various loads and observe the forces that will shake their structure until it collapses.

> The eighth grade curriculum gives students the ultimate task of designing and constructing CO_2 dragsters. They learn that one of the most important considerations automobile engineers focus on when designing a vehicle is aerodynamics. Aerodynamics involve how air flows past an object or how an object moves through air. Students use the design process to learn the relationship between friction, drag, and weight. They collaborate in groups of three or four to design a dragster that will have a low drag when placed in a wind tunnel and a high speed when raced on a 40-foot track. Since the construction of the vehicle is not a linear process, revisions are encouraged and expected; this helps students realize the importance of analyzing and modifying a design to achieve success.
>
> As you can see, school and district leaders can enhance education environments for students by supporting forward-thinking STEM programs. Brad's leadership and ability to recognize the importance of offering an Innovation and Design program provided students with collaborative, real-world educational experiences. Every student in the building takes these nine-week courses during each year of their middle-school experience. The opportunity to learn and construct while integrating technology excites students year in and year out. As Benjamin Franklin once said, "Tell me and I forget, teach me and I remember, involve me and I learn." More information related to the Innovation and Design classes can be found by emailing Brad at brad.currie@gmail.com.

From Brad's story we can see ways in which he help support his students and teachers incorporate STEAM, STEM and Making into their daily education routines. Brad is just one of many leaders who allow their teachers and educators to bring in new and innovative ideas. We also saw this in chapter 2 with Glenn Robbins who allows his students to play with computers in the hallways, to allowing students to learn about STEAM in indoor recess from Billy's Principal Sharon Tomback. These are ways in which an administrator can be supportive of the learning that takes place in the school.

Family

Families are a great resource for any STEAM program. As mentioned in chapter 3, families can be a great source of material donations for your program. Think beyond that, though. Having family buy-in to the STEAM program can make it more appealing to administration, and can also help sustain the program over the long term.

Your families can also be a source of expertise. Survey your students to see what professions their family members work in. Go beyond just immediate family! Perhaps there is someone with expertise that ties in with a unit you are planning. Reach out and see if they are willing to come visit the class to share that expertise. Doing a unit on the human body? Are there any families with member working in the medical field who can share what they know and answer questions? Doing a unit on Earth science? Are there any geologists among your students' families? Keep in mind that families can contribute in more ways than just a classroom visit. It can be hard coordinating work schedules with teaching schedules, so why not offer a chance to Skype into the classroom during a predetermined time? If a physical or virtual meeting is not possible, how about having students put together a list of questions to send via email for an asynchronous Q&A session?

A great way to introduce families to the STEAM program and to start gathering information about volunteers and resources is to host a Family STEAM Night. This is a fun and easy way to both show families what the program is all about, and to generate support. This event can be as simple or complex as you want. When Meredith launched the STEAM program at her first school, she hosted a STEAM Night one month into the program. Activity stations were set up in the STEAM lab and throughout the main lobby and art room, which were manned by both fellow teachers and students. Each station had a simple hands-on STEAM activity that was run by the teacher or student at the table. Flyers with information on the STEAM program and lists of donatable materials were handed out by other student volunteers. Families and community members were invited and had a chance to experience the STEAM program first hand and ask any questions they may have had. This event built up support for the new program and provided students with a way to take ownership of the new lab and program.

Community

Community involvement can really help launch and sustain your STEAM program. While families are a large part of your community, they are not all of it. There are many ways to get community members beyond families involved. As mentioned in earlier chapters, local stores and businesses can be a source of material donations and expertise for projects. The local hardware store may be willing to donate wood and other materials, while the local doctor's office may be able to send a nurse or other healthcare professional to speak with students during a unit on the human body. Don't forget to check in with your local town or county government for help as well.

In Meredith's current school, community involvement plays an even larger role. Every Tuesday, students run a shortened schedule of classes. After morning classes and a later-than-usual lunch, students spend the rest of the afternoon in mini-courses. These courses are two-hour blocks run by various members of the community. Students sign up for their preferred courses during a Mini Course Fair that is held three times a year, and spend ten weeks in each round of mini courses. These courses are developed and run by local groups, businesses, and even parents who are willing to come share their expertise with the students. A variety of courses are offered, from polymer play with the local science center, where students learn to make their own bioplastics, to a cosmetology course, to a computer programming course, and much more. These courses serve a variety of purposes. First, they give the students access to learn about areas of interest they may not come across during the regular course of school. Second, they provide professional development time on a weekly basis for the teachers – while students are in mini courses, the school staff is in PD each week. Thirdly, it is a great way for community members to become part of the school community and our program. Even if your school cannot commit to something like this during the school day, it can also be adapted easily to an after-school program.

Reflection Questions

- Who are some community members you can reach out to for help with your STEAM program? How will you approach them? What can they provide for your program?
- How can you bring your administration on board for a STEAM program?
- Who can you approach in your school or district to help you champion the move to STEAM education? How can they assist you?

8

Design Thinking
Taking Your STEAM Class to the Next Level

Changing Your Thinking with Empathy

As we defined earlier, Design Thinking is a relatively new term in the education world but is rapidly becoming a hot topic. Design Thinking is a way to bring empathy into the classroom by teaching students to use their STEAM and making skills to meet the needs of others, instead of just themselves. Students often use Design Thinking to help solve real-world problems for their communities and the wider world.

A book that was recommended to us as we started to develop the concept of this book was *A Whole New Mind* by Dan Pink. We referred to this book in the introduction and about how the world around us is changing as educators and we need to incorporate the right side of the brain and design into our teaching. In *A Whole New Mind*, Dan Pink writes:

> Design, that is, utility enhanced by significance – has become an essential aptitude for personal fulfillment and professional success for at least three reasons. First, thanks to rising prosperity and advancing technology, good design is now more accessible than ever, which allows more people to partake in in its pleasure and become connoisseurs of what was once specialized knowledge. Second, in an age of material abundance, design has

become crucial for most modern business – as a means of differentiation and as a way to new create markets. Third, as more people develop a design sensibility, we'll increasingly be able to deploy design for its ultimate purpose: changing the world.

Dan Pink has done an excellent job explaining here the importance of why we should focus on design in the business world. As educators, we need to take into account that we are teaching skills to our students for future jobs that might not even exist yet. We are no longer factory workers, as we mentioned in the introduction of this book. We need to help students develop skills such as using their right brains to think and create. Design Thinking is important for us to teach to our students and to have them develop not only design but also to understand that we need to teach our students about empathy. First, let's take a look at how the word "empathy" is defined:

Merriam-Webster defines empathy as:

1. The imaginative projection of a subjective state into an object so that the object appears to be infused with it.
2. The action of understanding, being aware of, being sensitive to, and vicariously experiencing the feelings, thoughts, and experience of another of either the past or present without having the feelings, thoughts, and experience fully communicated in an objectively explicit manner; also: the capacity for this.[1]

STEAM is for all students and as educators we need to plan to include everyone at every level. We have mixed learners in our classrooms, ranging from gifted and talented, to special education students, to our ever-growing English-language learners, let's also take a look at the meaning of "empathy" for English-language learners. Here is how Merriam Webster's defines "empathy" for English-language learners:

– the feeling that you understand and share another person's experiences and emotions

- ◆ He felt great empathy with/for/toward the poor;

– the ability to share someone else's feelings

- ◆ His months spent researching prison life gave him greater empathy towards/for convicts.[2]

We now have two definitions empathy but we should examine how Dan Pink defined it in his book *A Whole New Mind*. This is important because he discusses how design and empathy go hand in hand. In his chapter on empathy, he says "Empathy is a stunning act of imaginative derring-do, the ultimate virtual reality – climbing into another's mind to experience the world from that person's perspective." He goes on to discuss how empathy cannot be programmed into a computer in this new digital age we are a part of: "And the one aptitude that's proven impossible for computers to reproduce, and very difficult for faraway workers connected by electrons to match, is Empathy." Why bring all this up? Because it is more important than ever to teach our students empathy. We need to give students experiences that not only teach life skills but that also demonstrate how to connect with others in ways that computers and rote memorization alone cannot do.[3]

Ready, Set, Design!

Before we get into the importance of incorporating empathy in STEAM, let's take a quick look at a simple design project that can be done as a warm up to incorporating empathy-driven design projects. "Ready, Set, Design!" is a quick and easy design activity from the Cooper Hewitt Smithsonian Design Museum. This activity gives student teams a broad design challenge, and a bag of everyday materials to design a prototype with. A great feature of this activity is that it can be completed in a single 35–40 minute class period.

To begin, the teacher sets up a paper bag for each team, with a handful of prototyping materials. These are simple materials such as paper clips, coffee filters, rubber bands, popsicle sticks, note cards, and other everyday items. There are no set rules as to what goes in the bag, but the general guidelines recommend two to three "structure" materials (such as popsicle sticks or straws), two or three "covering" materials (such as notecards or coffee filters), and two or three "connecting" materials (such as rubber bands or string). You can make each bag the same, or vary the contents for each team.

The second step is to prepare the design challenges. Cooper Hewitt provides several sets of sample challenges on their website for a variety of age levels. You can also create your own challenges to use with your students. The only guideline is that challenges should be very broad and open-ended. Some challenges might include "I need to get groceries up several flights of stairs" or "I need to keep my hands warm". As with the supply bags, teachers can choose to give all the teams the same challenge, or give each team a different one.

Once the bags and challenges are prepared, it's time to prepare the students. One of the keys to this activity is to give as little instruction as possible. The basic instructions that Meredith gives classes participating in this challenge are as follows: You are going to design a prototype of a product to meet the challenge you are given. You may use any of the materials in your bag. You can use all of them, but you don't have to. Materials can be modified in any way, but you do not get replacements if you make a mistake. Your prototype does not need to be actual size or use the actual materials. You may not use any other items (scissors, glue, tape, etc.) to create your prototype. Your design must not be something that already exists (for example: given the challenge "I need to keep my hands warm" you may not create gloves or mittens).

Meredith usually gives the students about five minutes of planning time at the beginning of the activity. Students are allowed to look at and handle their supplies, but may not start building yet. This time is used to discuss ideas with their team and settle on a final idea. After five minutes of planning, the students are given fifteen minutes of build time. This activity often creates a sense of frustration in students at the beginning, as they are positive that creating a prototype with just the materials given is impossible. By the end of the build time, however, all groups end up with a prototype.

The final step in this activity is the sharing and feedback stage. Each team has to share their prototype and describe what it is and how it works. They then have to answer questions about this item from their classmates. In Meredith's class, students would ask questions ranging from how it worked to what colors it came in. One student being questioned exclaimed, "Hey, this is like Shark Tank!" and the kids quickly became much more passionate about explaining their designs.

The "Ready, Set, Design!" activity is a great way to get students thinking creatively about the needs of others. When using the challenge "I need to get groceries up several flights of stairs," Meredith would encourage students to consider the scenario of an elderly person who lives on the top floor of an apartment building with a broken elevator. How can they help this person get their groceries to their apartment? Student designs ranged from a pulley system with large baskets for groceries, to a grocery cannon that would launch bags up the stairs, to a drone complete with app for your phone that would fly your groceries directly to your window.

Extraordinary Design

Now the question becomes, how do empathy and STEAM go hand in hand? For our students, we can define empathy as being aware of another person's feelings or experiences.[4] We can create experiences for our students. Meredith introduced Billy and many other educators to an amazing way of teaching students about Design Thinking.

Welcome to "The Extraordinaires Design Studio". This kit, which we both purchased, helps bring the concept of design thinking to our students. The design studio has different characters, called Extraordinaires, who the students have to design for. One of the key features of this tool is that each character has something special about them. The front of the character cards give students a "first impression" of the character, but the back of the card gives a deeper insight into the character and their life. For example, the Alien character card shows a gigantic alien who looks like he is attacking a city. He's as tall as the buildings around him, people are running in fear, and he is zapping people with his ray gun. When asked for their first impressions of the character, students usually respond with adjectives such as "scary" or "evil". Turn the card over, however, and it tells a whole different story. We learn that although the alien seems gigantic and scary to us, among his own people he is actually a young child. The scenes on the back of the card show that he was visiting Earth on a class trip, and also show him displaying the humans he caught on his trip as part of show-and-tell! Now we realize that our first impressions can be wrong. We also need to consider how our design will reflect the fact that our alien is a child, not an adult, and that he has eight tentacles instead of arms and legs. Each of the characters in The Extraordinaires has a "twist" like this. There is a vampire teenager who does parkour through the city at night, but is bullied at school because he dresses like a stereotypical emo kid. The pirate has a hook for a hand, which means students need to consider how their design could be used by someone with a prosthetic.

The Extraordinaires also includes sets of design-challenge cards, with some of the smaller kits providing challenges in a single category, and the larger kit containing multiple categories, such as gadgets, buildings, vehicles, and more. There are also "Think" cards which provide open-ended questions to encourage the use of research skills and more. Combined, these tools provide an in-depth way to introduce students to empathy-driven design.

Billy has used The Extraordinaires Design Studio Pro with his third grade students and his gifted and talented students. They all loved doing design challenges for their Extraordinaire. There are ways in which you can easily modify the program to meet the unique aspects of your classroom. For instance, due to time issues Billy has only given one challenge to his students or has helped guide them during the design project. Students were given one of "The Extraordinaires" along with one of the Design cards. They were then told that they have ten minutes to discuss what the design was among themselves and twenty minutes to design and create. Students are given pencils and paper in order to complete this task. The students are told they are not building anything, but like any good designer they need to first come up with a sketch in order to see what the idea would look like. Students have five minutes at the end to present their ideas to the class. This is just a quick lesson that Billy has used to introduce his students to the whole Design Thinking concept.

Meredith has used "The Extraordinaires" with her students as part of a unit on Design Thinking. This design activity took place over the course of about two weeks, and had multiple stages. Each class formed into teams of four to five people, and each team received an Extraordinaire customer and a design challenge. During the first class period, we discussed their customer and their needs. The students were asked to brainstorm individually as many ideas as they could come up with to meet the design challenge they had been given. On the second day, students shared their brainstorm ideas with their teammates. This gave every student a chance to contribute something to the pool of ideas for their challenge. The teams were then instructed to use the brainstorm ideas to develop a team design. Meredith encouraged them to avoid choosing just one student's design, but rather to incorporate the best parts of each person's design into the final product. Students could also use their Chromebooks to research information for their design plans. One of Meredith's favorite moments in this lesson occurred during the research and design phase. While circulating the classroom and checking in with the teams, she spotted one team that had all of the members huddled intently around one Chromebook. Concerned that the students might be off-task, she checked in with the group to ask what they were doing. "Researching!" said one student. The students had been tasked with creating an underwater vehicle for a Merman. These fourth graders, without any prompting, had decided that in order to make the best design possible, they needed to research the PSI at different depths of the ocean so that they would know how much pressure the vehicle would need to withstand. "And then, Ms. M, we're going to research how much PSI different materials can take so we know what we would build it out of if we were making it for real!" This moment went far beyond the requirements of the lesson, but was a perfect example of student-driven inquiry and engagement.

Day three was spent giving and receiving feedback. Each team had to meet with at least two other teams to share their design ideas. They had to get and give feedback and then refine their designs based on the feedback. Once the team had their final design idea, they spent days four and five creating a formal design sketch of their product. The class had a short lesson on technical drawing and learned how to show a design from multiple views and how to annotate a design. Students then created full color, detailed drawings of their design. Final design sketches were approved by Meredith before students moved on to their favorite step, prototyping!

The prototyping stage took place over several days. Students had access to a variety of everyday materials, from construction paper to craft foam, cardboard tubes to cotton balls, yarn, bottles, craft sticks, and much more. One of the best parts of prototyping is that you rarely need any set types of materials, but can use everyday items from around the classroom. It was amazing how much effort students put into their prototypes. There was a high level of detail, and you could tell the students took great pride in their work.

The project does not end with the completion of the prototype. It is important that students be able to communicate and share information about their creations. During the course of the projects, students recorded their brainstorming, feedback, and day-to-day progress in a digital design journal that let them look back over their work and track their progress. At the end of the project, students presented their prototypes to the rest of the class. Their presentation needed to include a description of their design and how it met the needs of their Extraordinaire customer. The team also had to field questions from the class about their project and design choices, and defend those choices if necessary. It is important to note that students had a variety of choices as to how to present their design. Some chose to speak live in front of the class, some students created an advertising campaign for their design and still others used Screencastify to create a commercial video for their product. Student choice in how they presented had two benefits. First, students were able to choose a medium that was comfortable for them to work with and gave them some creative freedom. Second, Meredith was not forced to sit through dozens of virtually identical slideshows!

Design thinking can be more than just using the Extraordinaires, it is a process similar to the Engineering Cycle that is part of the Next Generation Science Standards. If you're not ready or able to purchase the Extraordinaires kit, there are many other ways to begin to incorporate empathy with design thinking. One great (free!) activity comes from Jackie Gerstein (www.makereducation.com): The MakerEd Card Game. This downloadable card game pairs students with a thing or process, a product to design, and a population to design for. Use the provided cards, or design your own to add to the game.

Another method of incorporating empathy that usually results in increased student engagement as well is taking Design Thinking out into your community. In Meredith's class, the next lesson after the Extraordinaires unit was based around neighborhood improvement. Students went on a neighborhood walk and explored several blocks around their school. During the walk, they were asked to identify things in the neighborhood that could be changed, added, or improved in order to make life better for their community. Students then used the design process back in the classroom to develop their ideas and create their presentations. Final projects ranged from a park that had both playground equipment for kids and a Wi-Fi-enabled gazebo for adults so that parents could come out and spend time with their kids and still be able to get work done; to a snowblower-type product that would clear snow from sidewalks and streets, but instead of piling it up would instead melt it down, purify it, and create clean drinking water for the community. Activities like this can be done on a large or small scale. Can't go out in the community? Look for ways to improve or change the school or classroom!

Reflection Questions

- How can you begin to incorporate empathy into your STEAM lessons?
- How will your students benefit from it?
- How will your community benefit from it?

Notes

1. "Empathy." *Merriam-Webster*, Merriam-Webster, www.merriam-webster.com/dictionary/empathy. Accessed 12 Apr. 2017.
2. "Empathy." *Empathy – Definition for English-Language Learners from Merriam-Webster's Learner's Dictionary*, www.learnersdictionary.com/definition/empathy. Accessed 12 Apr. 2017.
3. Pink, Daniel H. *A Whole New Mind*. New York: Riverhead Books, 2012. Print.
4. "Definition of Empathy – Merriam-Webster's Student Dictionary." *Definition of Empathy – Merriam-Webster's Student Dictionary*, www.wordcentral.com/cgi-bin/student?book=Student&va=empathy. Accessed 12 Apr. 2017.

9

Next Steps

Where Do We Go from Here?

By now, we've covered everything from planning to launching a STEAM space, to stocking it, to getting families and communities involved, and everything in-between. It's time to take this information and start to use it to plan out your own STEAM program. While we have made an effort to cover as much as possible in this book, there are still so many great resources out there. In this chapter, we'll talk about some excellent website resources for STEAM teachers and students, introduce you to some STEAM and maker communities online, and share our favorite places to get STEAM supplies from.

Takeaways and Resources

Websites

Instructables
Instructables (www.instructables.com) is one of Meredith's favorites for STEAM resources. This free, crowdsourced website allows anyone to upload instructions on how to do just about anything. Whether you are looking for recipes for dinner, crafts for your home, or lessons for a STEAM class, Instructables has you covered. The site also has a section dedicated to teachers and education (www.instructables.com/teachers/) with activities sorted by grade level and subject area. Instructables also has a large

selection of online classes you can register for, many just for the cost of the materials you will need to follow along. Instructables has both free and premium accounts, and they offer their premium accounts at no charge to teachers and students. Simply visit their teachers' section to sign up. Another benefit of the Instructables site, beyond finding lessons and activities to use with your students, is the ability to write and publish your own instructables. This can be a great way to include a language-arts component in your lessons, by having students write their own step-by-step instructions on how to complete a STEAM lesson and publish them to the site. We highly recommend taking some time to browse the activities on Instructables and find some awesome activities to do with your students. One of Meredith's favorite sources of STEAM lessons on Instructables is the Oakland Toy Lab (www.instructables.com/member/The%20Oakland%20Toy%20Lab/). Their activities are engaging, educational, and well written.

PBS Design Squad

The PBS Design Squad (pbskids.org/designsquad/) is another favorite source of STEAM activities and lessons we have shared a few resources of this amazing site in previous chapters. This website, funded in part by the National Science Foundation, has a wealth of kid-friendly STEAM activities. Kids can browse the site for videos, design challenges, things to build, and more. The best part for educators, however, is their teacher and parent section (www.pbskids.org/designsquad/parentseducators/) that includes a wonderful set of guides (including several created in conjunction with NASA); lesson plans in categories that include electricity and circuits, green design, helping others, and more; as well as training and information on how to set up a Design Squad club. Many of the lessons include downloadable handouts for both students and teachers, and a growing number of them also include Spanish versions for ESL students.

Makerspaces.com

Makerspaces.com is the perfect starting place for information on makerspaces, but much of the information there can be applied to STEAM as well. One of the best resources on the website is their free ebook on *Makerspace Resources*. Their blog has a great selection of posts on projects, products, ideas, and more.

Extraordinaires

We mentioned the Extraordinaires (www.extraordinaires.com/) in Chapter 8, and they definitely deserve a second look. These deceptively simple kits are perfect for helping your students develop empathy as part of their STEAM skills. The Extraordinaires guide children from designing things for themselves to designing things to meet the needs of others. Their website contains a ton of resources for educators that can be used along with any of their kits. From small individual kits to the all-inclusive Design Studio Pro, there are Extraordinaires kits for any classroom. Be sure to check out their education section (www.extraordinaires.com/education) for guides, lessons, and more.

D.school
The d.school (dschool.stanford.edu/) at Stanford is another superb resource for those interested in incorporating Design Thinking into their STEAM program. Their website provides a deeper dive into Design Thinking and includes a large selection of resources (dschool.stanford.edu/resources) for educators and students. Their resources pages include everything from an Empathy Planner, to design-project guides, to a reading list, and much more.

Pinterest
Pinterest.com is a great place to get ideas for storage, STEAM, STEM and maker lessons. If you search on Pinterest for STEAM, STEAM, STEM or MakerEd you will find thousands of different Pins in order to help you find an idea or use an idea that is already being used. Billy and Meredith have set up some Pins for you to already follow; check them out: https://pin.it/l54n4y6lv5x4yr and www.pinterest.com/yfandes/edu-steam/?lp=true.

#STEM, #STEAM, and #Makerspace
One of the most useful tools for creating a successful STEAM program is having access to a community of like-minded educators. Twitter is one way to build a PLN of other teachers and administrators with an interest in STEAM. There are tons of related hashtags out there to follow, but three of the largest and most established are #STEM, #STEAM, and #Makerspace. Following one or all of these hashtags will provide you with plenty of resources, ideas, and people to share with.

MakerPromise
MakerPromise (makerpromise.org) is a relatively new organization that is part of MakerEd and Digital Promise. Educators can sign up for free and receive access to resources, professional development, and opportunities. MakerPromise is also partnering with the Edcamp Foundation to host STEAM and maker-oriented Edcamps. Be sure to check out their sister site, Digital Promise (digitalpromise.org) for even more resources and

information, including micro-credentials. They have micro-credentials for STEM, Design Thinking, Maker Education, and more. Many of the micro-credentials can also be used to earn graduate credits!

MakerEd

MakerEd (makered.org) is another great community for makers and STEAM educators. Their resource library covers professional development, tools, types of spaces, and much more. One excellent resource on their site is the Events section, where you can find out about upcoming opportunities to learn and share with other educators.

Supplies

Adafruit and Sparkfun

Finding STEAM specific supplies and resources in traditional school supply catalogs, or even in your neighborhood stores can be difficult and costly. Thankfully, there are two great sources of STEAM specific materials. Adafruit (www.adafruit.com) and Sparkfun (www.sparkfun.com and sparkfuneducation.com) are well known in the STEAM community as your go-to places for both supplies and ideas. From Micro:bits to MakeyMakeys, Arduinos to accessories, you can find virtually everything you need for small electronics and projects. Both companies are very educator friendly and have plenty of projects, resources, and support for teachers and students.

Ozobot and Sphero

Ozobot (ozobot.com) and Sphero (www.sphero.com) are two excellent entrylevel robots for a fledgeling STEAM program. Ozobots are perfect for younger students in the preschool to first grade range, and Spheros for grades two and up. Both companies have a strong educational side and provide resources and lesson ideas for their robots.

MakeyMakey

The MakeyMakey is a fantastic tool that allows your students to become inventors. This simple circuit board attaches to any computer and allows you to turn any conductive item into a controller. Your kids can expand their creativity while learning about circuits and programming. Check out makeymakey.com for more information, and be sure to take a look at the *20 MakeyMakey Projects For The Evil Genius* book as well! (www.amazon.com/20-Makey-Projects-Evil-Genius/dp/1259860469)

Micro:bit

Ready to move up from the MakeyMakey? The BBC Micro:bit (microbit.org) is the next step in your physical computing toolkit. Learn to program with LEDs, sensors, Bluetooth, and radio, or expand even more with expansion kits and the built-in input/output rings. This little tool is extremely scalable, with simple drag and drop block coding options for younger students and JavaScript and Python programming options for those students ready to level up.

3D Printers

3D printers are becoming a popular tool in many STEAM classrooms these days, and they are definitely becoming more affordable. There are a plethora of brands to choose from based on your needs, so do your research before committing to a purchase. Some of the brands we recommend are the Monoprice (www.monoprice.com), Printrbot (printrbot.com), Lulzbot (www.lulzbot.com), Flashforge (flashforge-usa.com), and Dremel (digilab.dremel.com).

Finch Robots

The Finch robot (www.finchrobot.com) is an excellent robot that moves beyond the basics of Spheros and Ozobots. The Finch has a variety of sensors including an accelerometer, light sensor, temperature sensor, and obstacle sensor. It also has a pen mount for adding some art to your programming. The Finch can be programmed with a variety of tools and languages, and is scalable for students from age 5 to high school!

Want More Information About STEAM?

Check out these educators who are active on social media:

@SamPaute

@nathan_stevens

@DrStaubSTEM

@kjarrett

@pottsedtech

@davezirk

@dandanscience

@danielscrib

@DrTimony

@garystager

@brainbits

@MinecraftTeachr

@knowclue

@mr_isaacs

@PCSTech

@AFMulloy

@smelvin

@campbellartsoup

@fuglefun

Reflection Questions

- How will you continue your learning on social media?
- How will you continue your learning through the recommended sites?

10

Conclusion

Throughout this book, we have covered topics from the where, what, and why of STEAM to integrating STEAM across the curriculum. We hope you have come away with a better understanding of how to implement STEAM lessons in your own classroom. We hope you used the reflection questions as a way to improve your instructional practice and will find ways to take some the strategies we shared in this book and implement them into your teaching practice.

To wrap things up, we thought we would close with eight qualities of a teacher leader that are essential to creating and maintaining a strong STEAM program in your school or classroom.

Quality #1

Teacher leaders are those who can mesh strong pedagogical teaching practices with innovative tools to meet the needs of diverse learners in a STEM or STEAM environment.

In this particular case, a strong STEAM or STEM teacher is someone who is able to connect with students, embrace failure as a learning opportunity, leverage technology to foster a collaborative learning environment, and put students in a position to understand the connection between science, technology, engineering, arts and mathematics. In most cases, STEAM programs are new to a particular school or district. Most schools have talented staff members that can teach "outside of the box" and really make a STEAM class enjoyable for all.

Quality #2

Teacher leaders should take advantage of their PLN (Personal or Professional Learning Network) in order to provide the necessary resources to make the program the best it can possibly be.

Social media sites such as Twitter, Pinterest, Facebook, Google+, and Voxer have connected educators on a global scale. On a daily basis, best practices are tweeted, posted, pinned, or voxed. The more educators share best practices, the better the chance that student success will be impacted. Take for example the #stem and #steam hashtags. On any given day, innovative educators are sharing ideas, lesson plans, and resources related to science, technology, engineering, and math. School leaders must recognize the power of PLNs and how they can arm staff with knowledge that keeps them ahead of the game.

- Check out Jerry Blumengarten's, aka Cybraryman, website on all things STEM: www.cybraryman.com/stem.html;
- Follow the #STEM hashtag on Twitter:https://twitter.com/search?f=tweets&q=%23STEM&src=typd or https://twitter.com/search?f=tweets&vertical=default&q=%23STEAM&src=tyah;
- Are you a Google+ fan? Check out the STEM and STEAM Teachers Communities. It's also recommended that you follow the #stem hashtag when finding or sharing resources on Google+.

Quality #3

Teacher leaders secure school monies and grant opportunities to sustain and improve a STEAM program.

Starting and maintaining a successful STEAM program costs money. Teacher leaders can help by securing grant funding and finding other ways to help fund their STEAM program.

Websites such as www.donorschoose.org or www.grantwrangler.com put educators in touch with opportunities that support their STEM programs. From a local perspective, educational foundations and Parent Teacher Organizations (PTOs) can help with purchasing supplies to start a makerspace or possibly buy a 3D printer. BASF gives back to schools through annual $5,000 grants. Read on to learn more: www.basf.com/us/en/company/news-and-media/news-releases/2014/11/P-13-700.html.

Quality #4

Teacher leaders promote an environment of risk taking and failure. A key component of successful STEAM programs is living by the belief that "failure is an option."

Patience is a virtue. STEAM programs offer so many wonderful learning opportunities for students. School leaders must model risk taking and the acceptance of failure. We do not work in the perfection business, rather the improvement business. As students collaborate and problem-solve during STEAM activities things will not always work out. The teacher and students must know that it is perfectly fine for things to fall apart every once in a while. This mindset set comes from the top and must be communicated on a daily basis. Differentiating learning experiences and providing students with a multitude of ways to show what they know will help promote their success. For example, during a unit on solar power students should have the option to build a solar-powered car, house, helicopter, or other object where appropriate. This sort of autonomy will increase buy-in and excitement toward the subject matter.

Quality #5

Teacher leaders stress the importance of writing across the curriculum, particular in the STEAM setting.

Reading and writing in non-tested subject areas is critical if students are to receive a well-rounded education. As students learn in a STEAM environment, they also need to articulate, reflect, and assess their understanding. Writing for reflection and reading to stay current with trends in the STEAM world are very important. Teachers throughout the country are leveraging the power of Chromebooks and Google Drive in order to write in the digital world.

Quality #6

Teacher leaders support an interdisciplinary learning experience outside of science, technology, engineering, and mathematics – for example, incorporating art and social studies into the curriculum.

The STEAM movement is a hot-button topic in education. Science, technology, engineering, arts, and mathematics make a great team and do wonders for getting students to learn in an innovative environment.

STEAM classes also lend themselves to highlighting historical time periods as students comprehend how certain things came to be. Studying the history of Roman aqueducts, for example, can help students gain a grasp of what it took to build these great marvels.

Quality #7

Teacher leaders promote the story of their school or classroom's STEAM program through social media, information sessions, media outlets and the like. If you do not tell your school's story, someone else will, and it might be wrong. Leveraging the power of social media and various Web 2.0 tools will move good schools to great.

- Check out https://twitter.com/WantaghSTEAM as they share what they do daily.
- Check out Black River Middle School's Twitter handle to see how they tell their STEM program's story: https://twitter.com/blackriverms.
- Laura Fleming, teacher at New Milford High School in New Milford, NJ, maintains a tremendous web page titled "Worlds of Learning" to tell her classroom's story. It can be accessed here: http://worlds-of-learning.com.

Quality #8

Teacher leaders engage stakeholders, community members and parents in order to make the STEAM program more well-rounded and tangible.

All school districts have talented stakeholders who are willing to contribute at a moment's notice. Tapping into the experience of a parent who is an engineer or coder can do wonders for building up a student's excitement toward science, technology, engineering, and mathematics.

Inviting parents and community members into your school for Career Day to speak about STEAM career opportunities can be so beneficial. Also, conducting a mystery Skype or Google Hangout with people from the STEM industry will give students a more well-rounded perspective. Host a STEAM night and have parents participate in activities that their students do.

Reflection Questions

- What qualities do you see yourself embodying?
- What qualities can you add or improve upon to grow as a teacher leader?

Appendix
Sample Projects and Lesson Plans

SAMPLE PROJECTS

Sample Project 1: Punkin' Chuckin' Challenge

One of Meredith's favorite fall challenges is the Punkin' Chuckin' Challenge. Students love building catapults and competing to see who can launch their pumpkin the farthest. This challenge incorporates all aspects of STEAM. For science, it explores the concepts of levers and force. Technology can be included by using computers to collect and graph data, but remember that technology can also be the catapults themselves and the creation of them. Engineering is used in the design and construction of the catapults, and art can be seen in multiple parts of this project from the art of designing a catapult, to the history behind catapults, to a more literal art created using catapults and paint! A discussion of angles and measurement, along with collecting and comparing data pulls in the math component.

This project requires only a few simple items. Most can be found in the classroom or can easily be purchased at a dollar or craft store at minimal cost. The main items needed are popsicle sticks, rubber bands, plastic spoons, masking tape, paper plates, markers, and mini candy pumpkins. (If you cannot find these, any small projectile will do – try ping-pong balls, pom-poms, or small pieces of sponge.)

Students began by watching a video on the Punkin' Chuckin' Contest. Following the video, the class discussed the basics of levers. The class talked about how they could use the principles of a lever to design a catapult. Meredith modeled a simple catapult construction using popsicle sticks, rubber bands, masking tape, and a plastic spoon and the class measured the distance the catapult chucked the pumpkin. Since the catapults were small scale, students used small candy pumpkins instead of real ones.

Students were then challenged to design their own catapults and test them for distance and accuracy. Targets were created using the paper plates, with a bullseye marked in the center. The targets were placed 10 centimeters from the launch point for the catapults. The launch point was marked on the floor with masking tape to provide a definitive point to measure from.

At the beginning of the build time, students were given the following directions: *You have been given a supply of popsicle sticks, rubber bands, masking tape, and a plastic spoon. Using only these items, can you design a catapult to chuck your pumpkin the farthest? Can you make the most accurate catapult? Use what you have learned about levers to create your catapult. When it is complete, test it and measure your results. Then go back and see if you can improve your design. Record the results of the redesign and compare to the first results.*

Tips

- Does the size of the angle affect the distance? The accuracy?
- Does the amount of effort applied affect the distance? The accuracy?
- You may want to sketch your designs first!

Students used the following data collection chart to keep track of their results. The results could then be easily graphed and compared, both as individuals and as a class (Table A1).

Points: 1 point per centimeter your pumpkin travels – 5 points for hitting the target – 10 points for a bullseye.

After the challenge, students were asked to write about and reflect upon their experience. The writing needed to include the following sections:

- Describe the planning process. What did your team discuss while planning your build? How did you decide what type of catapult to build?
- What was the biggest challenge you faced during the build, and how did you overcome it?
- How successful was your catapult? Describe how you built it, and include your scores.
- If you could go back and redesign your catapult, what would you change and why?
- Be sure to include introductory and closing paragraphs.

Table A1 Sample student data collection chart

Catapult	Distance	Target	Bullseye
Test 1			
Test 2			
Test 3			
Average			

A great follow-up for this activity is catapult art. Set up a large canvas, such as a large piece of craft paper or an old bedsheet so that it hangs vertically. Have students create their catapults, and use pom-poms dipped in poster paint to launch at your canvas. Not only does this make a great abstract art lesson, but you can also add in a conversation about the forces of gravity.

This challenge has many variations and is very flexible. The main teacher responsibilities are dividing students into groups, providing the materials, and monitoring the project.

- *Group Size* – While three students per group is ideal (you will always have a tie-breaker), you may also have larger groups based on class size and makeup.
- *Materials* – Try this challenge with both limited and unlimited materials! You may want to run the challenge with unlimited materials the first time, then do a second round where you limit the number of materials they can use.
- *Expansion* – Instead of or in addition to the writing portion, students can create a presentation about their project to share with the class. Students can then go back and redesign based on what they learned from the presentations of their peers. You may also want to try the challenge with different materials. What types of catapults can they create with the addition of plastic cups? Old soda cans? Try out different items in the classroom and see what they can create!

A colleague of Meredith and Billy – Mark Grundel – used the catapult project as part of a larger activity that incorporated zombies! Students not only had to build their catapults, but then had to figure out how to make them work within an enclosed town created to defend it against a zombie attack.

Another aspect to keep in mind when planning a STEAM lesson is incorporating the engineering design process. For Sample Project 2, the engineering design process can be incorporated into the phases he used to teach the students. Those phases were: Planning Phase, Creation Phase, Testing Phase, Evaluation Phase.

Sample Project 2: Car Challenge

As we discussed in chapter 5, the Car Challenge, is a project in which students can apply some of the engineering skills they have learned. Tell students that they need to create a new car that must be powered without polluting the environment. The materials that students need are: toilet-paper tube, paper

Table A2 Car challenge data sheet

Car Data	
	Distance Traveled on Floor
Test 1	
Test 2	
Test 3	

towel tube, flexible straw, bottle caps, play dough, gloves, plastic bag, rubber bands, straws, paperclips. Let students know that they will NOT get any extra materials. To help you plan, please find the enclosed worksheets (Table A2).

Questions to Think About
How can you get the car to move?
How do you get the car to stay together using the materials you have?

Planning Stage
Meet as a team and discuss how you can create a car out of the materials you have. Then develop and agree on a design for your car.

Design (add a table to for the students to create their design below)

Materials Needed
(students should write in the materials that they need.

Creation Phase
Build your car.

Testing Phase
Each team will test their cars.

Sample Project 3: Slime Suncatchers

What kid doesn't love slime? It's colorful, ooey-gooey, and makes a wonderful mess. Perfect for a STEM lab project! Slime may have become the bane of teachers recently, but it is also a great way to learn about polymers and their solid and liquid properties. We are also going to add in an art aspect by using the slime to make suncatchers.

Supplies:
- White or clear school glue
- Liquid starch
- Food coloring
- Spoon for mixing
- Measuring cups and spoons
- Bowl for mixing
- Small, flat bowl or lid for suncatcher – petri dishes work perfectly!
- Plastic baggies

1. Begin by mixing 1/2 cup of glue with 1/4 cup liquid starch.
2. Next, add food coloring to create your desired color.
3. Mix it well!
4. If it's too liquidy, add more glue, one or two tablespoons at a time. If it's too sticky, add more starch one tablespoon at a time. When you are happy with the consistency, pour it out and get messy with it!
5. After making the first color, make a few more in different colors so you can have very colorful suncatchers.

Once you have the colors you want, take small blobs of each and added them to your suncatcher container. Petri dishes are the perfect size and shape for making suncatchers, but any small, shallow container will do. Let them dry until they are about the consistency of the gel window clings you can buy. You can then peel them out of the container and stick them to the window, or leave them in the container if it is clear and hang them that way.

Sample Project 4: Crystallizing Watercolors

This was a fun (but messy) project, with some pretty awesome results.
You will need:

- Water
- Epsom salts
- Table salt
- Food coloring
- Small bowls or cups for mixing
- Paint brushes
- Paper

1. The paint is easy to make. In your bowl or cup, mix 1/2 a tablespoon of epsom salts, 1/2 a tablespoon of water, a pinch of table salt, and food coloring of your choice.
2. Next, stir the mixture well to dissolve as much of the epsom salts and table salt as possible. You may end up with some of it undissolved, but that's OK. Warm water will help you dissolve as much as possible into the water. This is also a great point to discuss terms like solution, saturation, and supersaturation with your students.
3. Now the fun begins. Grab your paper and paintbrush, and begin creating your art.
4. The trick with this is to make sure you add lots of paint. Your paper will get a bit soggy, so make sure you have a drying area for them.

As they dry, you should see crystals beginning to form. Once the paint is completely dry, you'll have an awesome work of art covered in multi-colored sparkling crystals! A magnifying glass or microscope can allow your students to take a closer look at the crystals that form. Are all the crystals the same size or shape? What causes the crystals to form? There are tons of great avenues for you and your students to explore.

Sample Project 5: Geodesic Domes

This project is a fun one for kids. Not only do they enjoy the engineering aspect of it, but they are amazed to see how much weight a geodesic dome can hold.

Materials:
1. Toothpicks
2. Gumdrops
3. A Geodesic Dome is a sphere-like structure composed of triangular pieces.

Use toothpicks and gumdrops to create a Geodesic Dome.

1. Begin with one gumdrop. Insert 5 toothpicks in it to make a star pattern.
2. Add a gumdrop to the end of each of the 5 toothpicks. Your original gumdrop will now be the apex, or highest point, of your dome.
3. Connect the 5 gumdrops with toothpicks to form a pentagon shape. This will become the top of your dome.

4. On each side of the pentagon, use 2 toothpicks and one gumdrop to form an equilateral triangle.
5. Finally, connect the points of your equilateral triangles with toothpicks to form the base of the dome.
6. Test the strength of your dome by gently stacking books on top of it.

How much weight can it hold compared to a cube? Why is there a difference?

Sample Project 6: Marshmallow Tower Challenge

The marshmallow tower challenge is a common team-building and engineering challenge. There are several different variations – here's ours!
Materials:

- Half a box of (uncooked) spaghetti per team of four or five students
- Half a bag of marshmallows per team (open the bag and let it sit overnight – as the marshmallows become stale they become stronger)

As a team, your goal is to build the tallest tower you can in the given time (Usually 10–15 minutes) using only the spaghetti and marshmallows you are given.

- You may break the spaghetti into smaller pieces if you wish.
- The more the marshmallow can grip the spaghetti, the stronger the joint.
- If there is a heavy load on a marshmallow, it may change shape until the joint fails, so be careful!
- Use shorter pieces of spaghetti or put in braces to strengthen squares and rectangles in your structure.
- Where you choose to use shortened pieces of spaghetti, make sure you cut them accurately. If you don't use pieces of equal length on each side, your tower may start to twist and topple.
- There will be most strain on the base of the tower – think about how you can add strength here.

Sample Project 7: Marshmallow Catapults

Catapults are a fun way to explore concepts such as angles, velocity, and measurement!

Materials:
- Craft sticks
- Rubber bands
- Plastic spoons
- Small items to launch (marshmallow, pom-pom, ping-pong ball, etc.)

1. Stack 6–7 craft sticks on top of each other, and rubberband tightly at each end.
2. Take two more craft sticks, lay them on top of each other, and rubber band them tightly at one end only.
3. Insert the first stack of craft sticks inside the two you just connected to form a cross.
4. Join the two pieces with a rubber band, wrapped in a criss-cross fashion.
5. Use a rubberband to attach a plastic spoon to the end of the upper craft stick.
6. LAUNCH!

Whose catapult launched the farthest? The highest? What variables in your design can you change to make your catapult throw farther or higher?

Sample Project 8: Saving Sam

This is one of Meredith's favorite intro lessons in the lab. It's wonderful for teaching teamwork and problem solving!

Materials:
- Gummy worm
- Gummy "Life Saver" preserver
- 1 Plastic or paper cup
- 4 Paper clips

Sam sits on the inverted cup. The cup sits half-covering the life preserver on the tabletop. No real water is involved.

Sam, the boat, and the life preserver can be touched only with the paper clips. NO HANDS.

Sam has been spending his summer boating on the great lakes. However, he's not too bright (after all, the brains of worms are pretty small). He's never learned how to swim, and he never wears his life preserver. The worst has happened! His boat has capsized and he's stuck! Fortunately, his life preserver is in the boat, but unfortunately he does not know how to reach it without falling off and drowning. How can you and your partner save Sam using only 4 paper clips. You may not touch Sam, the boat, or the life preserver directly with your hands.

Sample Project 9: Popsicle Stick Harmonica

Let's add some music to STEAM!

Materials:
- Popsicle sticks
- Rubber bands
- Paper
- Toothpicks
- Scissors
- Glue

Ready to make an instrument?

1. Begin by cutting a piece of paper the same length and width as your popsicle stick. This will act as a reed inside the instrument.
2. Next, cut a toothpick into two sections the width of your popsicle stick. You're going to put one toothpick piece on each end of the popsicle stick and stick them down with a little dot of glue.
3. Your paper strip can then be laid across the top of them.
4. Finally, lay your second popsicle stick on top, making a nice sandwich, and rubber band each end to hold it together.

Congratulations, you should now have a harmonica. Hold it to your mouth and blow gently.

Sample Project 10: Glowsticks

Glowsticks are a great project to introduce electricity and simple circuits! It's also a great way to reuse those old holiday lights that have few dead or missing bulbs.

Materials:
- 9-volt battery
- Battery snap cap
- String of holiday lights
- Electrical tape
- Scissors
- Wire strippers

1. Cut off the plug end of the lights and discard.
2. Cut a strip of four bulbs, leaving several inches of wire at each end.
3. Using the wire strippers, strip off about ¾ of an inch of the plastic covering from the wire at both ends.
4. Twist one end of the light string wire around one of the exposed wire of the battery cap, and wrap in electrical tape.
5. Repeat with the other end of the light string wire. and the remaining battery cap wire.
6. Attach the battery cap to the 9-volt battery to light your string up.
7. Enjoy!

Note: Please attach both wires and wrap the connections with electrical tape BEFORE connecting the battery to avoid a mild zap!

SAMPLE LESSON PLANS

Sample Lesson Plan 1: Easter Egg Genetics, Inherited Traits

Overview:
Offspring inherit their traits from their parents. Dominant and recessive genes determine which traits the offspring will show. In this lab, the parents are represented by plastic Easter eggs. Students will use punnett squares to determine possible offspring colors.

Objectives:
Using their knowledge of genetics and inherited traits, students will be able to identify potential offspring colors with punnett squares.

Materials
- Plastic Easter eggs in the following colors: purple, pink, yellow, blue, green, orange.
- Beads/tokens/jellybeans/etc that match the colors of the eggs.

- Tape (optional)
- Student worksheet
- Discussion questions

Lesson

The plastic eggs are the parents, with one half representing the female parent and the other half representing the male. Combine the egg halves and fill with the four beads representing the potential offspring colors using the Genotype/Phenotype Key. You may seal the eggs with tape if needed.

Each group of students (4–5 per group) should have all twelve color combinations. Have students choose one egg at a time (either individually or with partners) and, without opening the egg, use a punnett square and the genotype of the parents to predict the colors of the offspring. Students can self-check by opening the egg.

After completing the punnett square and checking their work, students should choose another egg and repeat the process until each student or pair have completed the punnett squares for at least five different eggs.

If you prefer, students can leave the eggs sealed until all the punnett squares are completed, and then the class can open the eggs and check their predictions as a group.

Students should then complete the discussion questions.
Teacher Notes
Egg Genetics Key (genotype/phenotype key)
PP=purple
pp=pink
Pp=orange
BB=blue
bb=yellow
Bb=green

Each genotype represents one half of an egg. For example, an egg that was one half purple and one half pink would be represented as PP × pp. A completely purple egg would be represented as PP × PP.

Genotype/Phenotype key:
Each group should have one of each of the following twelve combinations.
Genotype/Phenotype key:
Each group should have one of each of the following twelve combinations (Table A3).

Extensions/Modifications

- Reverse the activity. Give students the Egg Genetics Key and have them place the correct color of offspring in the eggs.

Table A3 Genotype/Phenotype key

Egg Combinations	Potential Offspring
purple x purple (PP x PP)	four purple (PP)
purple x pink (PP x pp)	four orange (Pp)
pink x pink (pp x pp)	four pink (pp)
orange x orange (Pp x Pp)	1 purple (PP), 2 orange (Pp), one pink (pp)
orange x purple (Pp x PP)	2 purple (PP), 2 orange (Pp)
orange x pink (Pp x pp)	2 orange (Pp), 2 pink (pp)
blue x blue (BB x BB)	four blue (BB)
blue x yellow (BB x bb)	four green (Bb)
blue x green (BB x Bb)	2 blue (BB), 2 green (Bb)
yellow x yellow (bb x bb)	four yellow (bb)
green x yellow (Bb x bb)	2 green (Bb), 2 yellow (bb)
green x green (Bb x Bb)	1 blue (BB), 2 green (Bb), 1 yellow (bb)

- Introduce a mutation possibility.
- Have students challenge each other to complete the punnett squares correctly the fastest.
- Have students determine the probability of offspring colors for a given set of parents.

Sample Lesson Plan 2: Bird Beak Adaptations

Overview
Bird beaks come in a variety of shapes and sizes. Special beak shapes help birds eat the different types of food in their environment. These beak shapes are considered adaptations. We will be testing different beak shapes on a variety of bird food to find which shapes work best with which types of food.

Objectives
1. Comprehend that birds have physically adapted in relation to their type of food supply.

2. Deduce which beaks are most efficient for given foods by experimenting with imitation beaks and given food sources.
3. Learn the importance of multiple trials.
4. Represent data with a bar graph.

Materials

- Three each of: eyedroppers, chopsticks, pliers, slotted spoons, and tweezers
- One thin vase
- Paper plates or bowls
- Two large saucepans
- Popcorn
- Rice
- Gummy Worms
- Oatmeal
- Walnuts (in shell)
- Plastic straws cut into small pieces
- Paper or plastic cups
- Introduction Bird Beaks video: http://youtu.be/XzHQ5-lYvrk
- Fit The Bill data collection worksheet (see Table A4)

Lesson

Introduction

The beaks of birds have adapted to enable different species to eat the foods available in their environment. For example, a hummingbird could not eat a mouse, and a hawk could not get nectar from a flower.

Watch and discuss the Bird Beaks video (http://youtu.be/XzHQ5-lYvrk).

Procedure

Students will navigate between five stations, each with "bird food" that fits a type of bird beak. They will create a hypothesis for each station as to which "beak" will work best, and then collect data. Students can work individually or in small groups.

Stations

Station 1

- Food – water in a thin vase
- Beaks – eyedropper, tweezers, slotted spoon

Table A4 Bird beak adaptations data sheet

Station 1 Food source _____	Beak 1 _____	Beak 2 _____	Beak 3 _____
Station 2 Food source _____	Beak 1 _____	Beak 2 _____	Beak 3 _____
Station 3 Food source _____	Beak 1 _____	Beak 2 _____	Beak 3 _____
Station 4 Food source _____	Beak 1 _____	Beak 2 _____	Beak 3 _____
Station 5 Food source _____	Beak 1 _____	Beak 2 _____	Beak 3 _____

Station 2

- Food – saucepan filled with oatmeal with Gummy Worms on the bottom
- Beaks – chopsticks, pliers, eyedropper

Station 3

- Food – whole walnuts
- Beaks – pliers, tweezers, slotted spoon

Station 4

- Food – straw pieces floating in saucepan of water
- Beaks – slotted spoon, eyedropper, chopsticks

Station 5

- Food – rice spread on a paper plate
- Beaks – tweezers, pliers, chopsticks

Student Directions
Pretend you are a bird. Each station has a different type of food, and three different "beaks". Make a hypothesis as to which beak will work best for that food type.

1. Write your hypothesis.
2. See how much food you can collect in your cup for each beak in 20 seconds.
3. Enter your data for each beak on your chart.
4. Repeat at each station.
5. Once you have collected data from all stations, we will average the class data and graph it for each station.

Once students have completed their data charts, have them share their numbers with the class. As a class, average the number for each beak at each station.

Graph the data either as a class or in small groups. Discuss which beak was best at each station and why. Ask students if their data matched their hypotheses and discuss.

Review how bird beaks adapted to fit their food source. Ask students if they can think of any other animals with adaptations to fit their environment, and discuss.

Fit the Bill Data Collection Worksheet

Extensions/Modifications
This activity can be done with more stations added (e.g.: small aquarium nets for catching airborne insects).

Instead of rotating through all of the stations, each group can be responsible for just one, and then pool their data as a class.

Expand the activity to discuss what types of habitats each food source represents and research the types of birds that would live there.

Sample Lesson Plan 3: Weather Fronts

Overview:
Students will learn about the types of weather fronts, and what happens when a front moves in. They will create a model of a weather front, and complete a digital lab.

Objectives
1. Students will be able to explain what a weather front is, and the main types of weather fronts.
2. They will explain what happens when different types of weather fronts appear.
3. They will identify the effect the different types of fronts have on the weather.

Materials:

Lab Materials – per group
- Clear glass cooking dish
- Blue food coloring
- Cooking oil
- Water
- Scissors
- Cardboard
- Plastic wrap

Virtual Materials
- Weather front animation: www.phschool.com/atschool/phsciexp/active_art/weather_fronts/index.html
- Weather Virtual Lab: www.edheads.org/activities/weather/frame_loader.htm

Lesson

Introduction
Ask students if they know what weather fronts are. Explain that they will be learning how warm and cold fronts affect the weather. Watch the Weather Fronts Study Jam video – http://youtu.be/tkK4_F0VKhM and discuss.
Overview

Explain that students will be creating a model weather front to show what happens when fronts collide. They will also be using an interactive lab to identify and forecast different types of weather.

1. Cut the cardboard so that it fits tightly across the middle of the glass dish. Wrap it with plastic wrap and seal tightly. Place the barrier across the centre of the dish, with it fitting as snugly as possible.
2. On one side of the barrier, add cooking oil until it nearly reaches the top.

3. Repeat with water on the other side, and add a few drops of food coloring.
4. When the liquids are calm, quickly lift the barrier and carefully observe what happens.
5. Explain to students that this lab illustrates what happens when a warm front meets and replaces a cold front. The oil represents the warm front, and the colored water represents the cold front. Oil is less dense than water, so similar to how warm air is less dense than cold air. When the two masses meet, the oil (warm air) rises over the water (cold air).
6. Direct students to the weather front animation – www.phschool.com/atschool/phsciexp/active_art/weather_fronts/index.html – and give them time to watch the weather front models.
7. Discuss what happens when different types of weather front meet.
8. Inform students that they will be completing a virtual lab on predicting weather, using what they have learned about weather fronts.
9. Direct students to the virtual lab – www.edheads.org/activities/weather/frame_loader.htm – and instruct them to begin the Predict The Weather module. Students will complete the lab individually.
10. When the virtual lab is completed, discuss what students have learned about predicting weather, and how warm and cold fronts can affect local weather.

Assessment

1. Define (in your own words) the following terms:
   a. Cold front
   b. Warm front
   c. Air mass

2. What types of weather are often associated with a cold front? A warm front?
3. Why does warm air rise over cold air?
4. How can knowledge of weather fronts help scientists predict the weather?
5. Draw a diagram showing and labeling a cold front.
6. Draw a diagram showing and labeling a warm front.

Extensions

Are there other types of weather fronts? How do they form and how do they affect the weather?

Have students use real-time weather data to predict future weather for various locations using resources such as NOAA – www.nws.noaa.gov/outlook_tab.php

Create a daily or weekly weather forecast video using real world data.

Sample Lesson Plan 4: Scale of the Solar System

Overview
When we look at traditional models of the solar system, the distances between planets do not seem that great. In reality, the planets are millions of miles apart. In this activity, we'll create a scale model to help show the immense distances between planets in our solar system.

Objectives
Students will be able to analyze and use data to model the scale of the solar system.

Materials
- 11 Sticks or dowels
- 1 Baseball
- Several grains of sand
- 1 – ⅜ inch ball
- – 2/8 inch ball
- – ⅛ inch balls
- Dust or flour
- Glue
- Measuring tape or yardstick

Preparation
Using the Planetary Scale chart, glue each planetary representation object to a dowel or stick except for the Asteroid Belt – this will be represented by the dust or flour being scattered on the ground. Print out and attach the Planet Data card to each one.

Lesson

Introduction
Have students share what they know about our solar system. Discuss as a class how far apart they think the planets are from the sun. Give students the Planet Facts handout and discuss. Explain that they are going to create a scale model of the solar system to help show the enormous size of interplanetary distances.

Procedure
In a large, open area outside (playground, park) have students begin by placing the stick representing the sun at the beginning location. Explain that you have scaled down the sizes to make it possible to walk between the planets at this scale.

Procedure
Using the measuring tape or yard stick, explain that we will be using yards as our measurement system. One yard is roughly equivalent to one large stride. Have students practice until they are comfortable making regularly spaced strides.

Begin walking the distances for the planets, using the Planetary Scale chart. All distances measure from the sun, NOT from the previous planet. At each stop, have students place the marker for that planet or object and fill in their data sheets. Continue until all objects have been placed (Tables A5–A7).

Student Questions
1. Are the distances between planets uniform?
2. Is there a pattern to the inter-planet intervals?
3. What was the most surprising thing you learned?
4. What was the most interesting thing you learned?

Sample Lesson Plan 5: Rebop Genetics

Overview:
Rebops are fictional animals used to teach about inheritance of genetic traits. Rebops have eight characteristics, and each has both a dominant and recessive trait. The offspring of Rebops show traits based on the genes they inherit from their parents. In this lesson, students will demonstrate how traits are inherited and design a 3D model of their Rebop offspring.

Objectives:
Students will apply the principles of genetic transfer.
They will design an offspring based on genetic information.
They will demonstrate the relationship between genotype and phenotype.

Materials
- Rebop Sire and Dam Traits handout – one of each per student or group[1]
- One coin per student

Table A5 Planetary scale

Solar System	Representative Object	Scaled Distance	Actual Distance (Millions of Miles)
Sun	Baseball	Center	0
Mercury	Grain of sand	5 yards	36
Venus	Grain of sand	9 yards	67.2
Earth	Grain of sand	13 yards	93
Moon	Grain of sand	1″ from earth	–
Mars	Grain of sand	20 yards	141.6
Asteroids	Dust or flour	33 yards	186–370
Jupiter	⅜″ ball	66 yards	483.6
Saturn	²/₈″ ball	122 yards	888.2
Uranus	⅛″ ball	247 yards	1,786
Neptune	⅛″ ball	348 yards	2,799
Pluto	Grain of sand	507 yards	3,666

Table A6 Planet data cards

Mercury	Venus	Earth
Period of revolution (year) – 87.97 days	Period of revolution (year) – 224.7 days	Period of revolution (year) – 365.26 days
Period of rotation (day) – 58.65 days	Period of rotation (day) – 243.01 days	Period of rotation (day) – 23 hrs. 56min
Diameter – 3,031 miles	Diameter – 7,521 miles	Diameter – 7,926 miles
Atmosphere – None	Atmosphere – Carbon Dioxide	Atmosphere – Nitrogen & Oxygen
Moons – 0	Moons – 0	Moons – 1
Rings – 0	Rings – 0	Rings – 0

(*Continued*)

Table A6 (Continued)

Mars	Jupiter	Saturn
Period of revolution (year) – 686.9 days	Period of revolution (year) – 11.86 years	Period of revolution (year) – 29.46 years
Period of rotation (day) – 24 hrs. 37 min.	Period of rotation (day) – 9 hrs. 56 min.	Period of rotation (day) – 10 hrs. 40 min.
Diameter – 4,219 miles	Diameter – 88,729 miles	Diameter – 74,975 miles
Atmosphere – Carbon Dioxide	Atmosphere – Hydrogen & Helium	Atmosphere – Hydrogen & Helium
Moons – 2	Moons – 16	Moons – 18
Rings – 0	Rings – 3	Rings – 1000+

Uranus	Neptune	Pluto
Period of revolution (year) – 84.07 years	Period of revolution (year) – 164.82 years	Period of revolution (year) – 248.6 years
Period of rotation (day) – 17 hrs. 14 min.	Period of rotation (day) – 16 hrs. 6 min.	Period of rotation (day) – 6.39 days
Diameter – 31,763 miles	Diameter – 30,775 miles	Diameter – 1,429 miles
Atmosphere – Hydrogen, Helium, & Methane	Atmosphere – Hydrogen, Helium, & Methane	Atmosphere – Methane
Moons – 17	Moons – 8	Moons – 1
Rings – 11	Rings – 5	Rings – 0

Asteroid Belt	Moon	Sun
Location – Between Mars and Jupiter	Distance to Earth: 238,900 miles	Diameter – 863,710 miles
Contains billions of asteroids.	Orbital period: 27 days	Composition – Hydrogen & Helium
We have only identified about 7,000 asteroids.	Age: 4.527 billion years	Age – 4.5 billion years old
The largest asteroid Ceres was the first to be discovered in 1801, it has recently been re-classified as a dwarf planet.	Circumference: 6,784 miles. From the Earth we can only see one side of the Moon; the other side is always turned away from us.	The biggest, brightest, and hottest object in our solar system.

Table A7 Student data sheet

Solar System	Scaled Distance	Actual Distance (Millions Of Miles)	Interesting Fact
Sun			
Mercury			
Venus			
Earth			
Moon			
Mars			
Asteroids			
Jupiter			
Saturn			
Uranus			
Neptune			
Pluto			

- Decoder Key – one per student or group
- Student handout – one per student
- Tinkercad.com or similar 3D modeling program
- 3D printer and filament
- Note: If 3D printing is not an option, modeling clay can be used instead

Vocabulary
- Genotype – genetic makeup
- Phenotype – physical appearance
- Heterozygous – genes are different: pair of dominant and recessive genes
- Homozygous – both genes are the same
- Dominant traits – a trait that will appear in the offspring if one of the parents contributes it (e.g.: DD or Dd)
- Recessive traits – recessive traits can be carried in genes without appearing (e.g.: dd)
- Additive traits – more than one gene that genetically codes for the same function (e.g.: DD = 0 antenna, Dd = 1 antenna, dd = 2 antennae)

Lesson

This lesson is best used after students have a basic understanding of genetic trait inheritance and have used punnett squares before.

Review genetics vocabulary with the students.

Introduce the lesson and explain that students will use what they have learned about genetic-trait inheritance to breed Rebops. They will receive two sets of genes, one from the sire and one from the dam. Using a coin, they will flip to determine dominant or recessive for each trait. They will then use these traits to create a genotype and phenotype for their offspring. Use the Rebop slideshow to demonstrate the process. Students will use the student handout to record their data.

Lesson

Once students have completed the genetics part of the lesson, they will design their Rebop in a 3D modelling program, being sure to match their phenotype. Tinkercad.com is a very simple 3D design program that is easy to learn and use. It also has built-in tutorials for those unfamiliar with 3D design. Any 3D design program, however, can be used. If access to 3D printers is not an option, students can use modelling clay as an alternative.

After printing, students will compare their offspring as a class and complete the writing activity.

Note: Students can work individually or in pairs on this project.

Extensions and Modifications

- Calculate the probability of each trait being expressed.
- Have students try to breed for specific traits over multiple generations.
- Create multiple sires/dams with different genotypes to breed from.
- Introduce mutations.
- Have students create a video or slideshow explaining how their Rebop acquired its traits.

Sample lesson plan 6: M&M adaptation: camouflage

Overview:

Animals adapt to their environment in many ways. One of the most common adaptations is camouflage, the ability to blend in with their environment. In this lesson, students will become predators hunting for prey – tasty M&Ms! It won't be as easy as it looks, since some of the M&Ms will use their camouflage to blend into their habitat.

Objectives:
Students will be able to explain adaptation.

They will describe how an adaptation such as camouflage can help animals survive.

Materials
- Per group

    o Six plastic sandwich baggies
    o M&Ms – ten of each color: yellow, blue, green, orange, red, brown
    o Skittles – 60 of each color: orange, yellow, green, red, and purple
    o Paper plate

- Timer or stopwatch – one per group if possible, or the teacher can be in charge of keeping time.

Set up:
- Place ten M&Ms of each color in ONE baggie for each group. Each baggie should have 60 M&Ms in total.
- For each group, place 60 Skittles in each of the remaining five baggies according to color. You should have 60 red Skittles in one bag, 60 green in another, and so on.

Lesson
Discuss animal adaptations with the class. Have students list adaptations that they know of. Explain that one common adaptation for many animals is camouflage. Camouflage helps animals blend in with their habitat. Share the camouflage slideshow with the class and have students take turns picking out the hidden animals. Discuss how the animals' camouflage helps them blend into their habitats.

Tell students that in this lab they will be predators hunting for their prey within their habitats. Some of their prey will have a camouflage adaptation. They will collect data to show if/how the camouflage protects the prey from predators.

Give each student a set of materials (one baggie of M&Ms, five baggies of Skittles, and a paper plate). Explain that the M&Ms are the prey, and the Skittles are their habitats.

Have students choose one bag of Skittles and pour it into the paper plate. Next, they can pour in their M&Ms and mix them with the Skittles.

Explain that they will be using their fingers like bird beaks to pick out their prey. They will have 20 seconds to get as many M&Ms as possible. Tell students that Skittles will make their predator sick, so they should focus on the M&Ms and avoid the Skittles.

At the end of 20 seconds, they will stop and record their data on their student worksheets, then duplicate the activity for each of the remaining Skittle colors.

If you have one timer or stopwatch, the teacher can keep time for each round. If each group has a timer, they can take turns being the timekeeper or a predator.

Remind students NOT to eat the candy during the activity, since the M&Ms will be reused for each habitat. You may choose to allow students to eat the candies at the end of the lesson if you wish.

After all rounds are complete, compare the data as a class and discuss what conclusions they can draw from it.

Extensions/Modifications

- As a class, group, or individuals, graph the results of the data and discuss.
- Repeat the lab with different types of candies for the habitats (Nerds, candy corn, etc.). How do different shapes or color patterns for the habitats affect the amount and colors of M&Ms collected?
- Choose an animal that uses camouflage and write a report on what their camouflage is and how it helps them in their habitat. Students can then present on their animals to the class.

You can show how adaptation can occur over generations by doubling the M&Ms left after predation (e.g.: if two green and one blue are left, add two more green and one blue). How many generations until you get all one color?

Note

1. Handouts and resources can be found at: https://drive.google.com/drive/folders/0B1fsVigeyeiLfmlybk1OdXFJaXdBSjBGT2o5MmNmUE1nRkhqOUFsWTAxOG5oZTMxTlRldDg?usp=sharing